# MAMA
# LEAH'S
# JEWISH
# KITCHEN

# MAMA LEAH'S JEWISH KITCHEN

*Leah Loeb Fischer*

with *Maria Polushkin Robbins*

*MACMILLAN PUBLISHING COMPANY*
*New York*

*COLLIER MACMILLAN CANADA* Toronto

*MAXWELL MACMILLAN INTERNATIONAL*
*New York Oxford Singapore Sydney*

Macmillan Publishing Company
866 Third Avenue, New York, NY 10022

Collier Macmillan Canada Inc.
1200 Eglinton Avenue East, Suite 200
Don Mills, Ontario M3C 3N1

Library of Congress Cataloging-in-Publication Data

Fischer, Leah Loeb.
Mama Leah's Jewish kitchen / Leah Loeb Fischer, with
Maria Polushkin Robbins.
p. cm.
ISBN 0-02-538461-9
1. Cookery, Jewish.    I. Polushkin, Maria.    II. Title.
TX724.F47 1990                                    90-34754
641.5'676—dc20                                         CIP

Design by Chris Welch

10 9 8 7 6 5 4 3 2
Printed in the United States of America

*In loving memory of my husband, Stan,*
*who always encouraged me in all my*
meshuggeh *endeavors.*
*L.L.F.*

# CONTENTS

## *Chapter 2*

□ □ □ □ □ □ □ □ □

## SOUP   *4 4*

## *Chapter 3*

□ □ □ □ □ □ □ □ □ □

## EGG DISHES  *7 8*

## *Chapter 4*

□ □ □ □ □ □ □ □ □ □

## GRAINS AND NOODLES  *8 4*

## *Chapter 5*

□ □ □ □ □ □ □ □ □

## BLINTZES, KNISHES, LATKES, VARENIKIS, AND OTHER GOODIES  *9 7*

### *Chapter 8*

□ □ □ □ □ □ □ □ □ □

## MEATS  *1 5 2*

## *Chapter 9*

□ □ □ □ □ □ □ □ □

# STUFFED VEGETABLES  *180*

## *Chapter 10*

□ □ □ □ □ □ □ □ □

# SALADS  *186*

## Chapter 11

□ □ □ □ □ □ □ □ □

### VEGETABLES *194*

## Chapter 12

□ □ □ □ □ □ □ □ □

### PASSOVER *204*

## *Chapter 13*

□ □ □ □ □ □ □ □ □ □

## BREADS AND BAGELS  *2 2 6*

## *Chapter 14*

□ □ □ □ □ □ □ □ □ □

## SWEETS  *2 3 6*

## AROUND THE KITCHEN TABLE:

## FINAL THOUGHTS FROM MAMA LEAH   *2 4 9*

# INTRODUCTION

Over the years people have asked me a lot of questions about myself and my cooking. For example, maybe you'd look at me and say, "Mama, were you born knowing how to cook—or did you have to learn like everybody else? How did you start?" Well, when I was eleven years old, right after the war started, my mother had to go to work. My sisters and I had to share the responsibilities of housekeeping, so I decided that I would do the cooking, my sister Shirley would clean the kitchen and the bathroom, and my sister Libby would do the bedrooms and the living room. Sounds reasonable, right? Forget about it! The fights we used to have were unbelievable. Every time I wanted to go in to do the cooking, Shirley would give a *geshrei* (a loud yell) and throw up her hands crying, "What kind of mess are you going to make in my nice clean kitchen? I just finished in there." My sister was crazy clean back then. She still is. But one way or another we would work it out and I would begin to cook. Basically I would try to remember what my

mother did, and when I couldn't, well, then maybe I would impro-
vise a little. And I would experiment on my father, who loved it.
That was the beginning—a little verbally colorful frustration from
my sisters to keep it interesting, and a lot of enthusiasm from my
father, Chaim, to encourage me. My mother, Esther, by the way,
was a great instinctive cook. She knew only from *schit arein,* that's
Yiddish for a little bit of this, a little bit of that. . . . Her only
measuring tool was a *yohrzeit* glass, you know, the glass for the
memorial candle. That measured everything she needed to measure and it was good for cutting out round shapes in dough as well.

You say, "Tell me, Mama, what is Jewish cooking? There seem
to be so many different opinions. Help me, I'm confused." No need
to be confused, *kinderle.* There are as many different kinds of
Jewish cooking as there are countries that Jews have been allowed
to live in, and since Jews have lived practically everywhere in the
world, you could find Jewish cooking in almost any kind of international cuisine. I myself am of an Eastern European background,
as, by the way, are a great many other Jews in America. So, to me,
Jewish cooking is the cooking that originated back in the Old
Country, in the shtetls of Russia, the Ukraine, Poland, Romania,
Lithuania, where many of our grandparents came from. The Jewish cooking that produced borscht and brisket, chicken soup and
knishes, matzo brei, latkes, and blintzes—that's the cooking that
I'll be writing about in this book.

I see you still look a little confused. Let me make it simple. In
Jewish cooking, particularly in the cooking that comes from
Mama Leah's Jewish kitchen, don't look for fancy-shmancy; don't
look for *nouvelle* anything; and don't look for gourmet. My
mother's idea of a gourmet was someone who was a picky eater.
Don't expect to find steaks that are bloody rare, chicken still pink
inside, or fish that's raw—because Jews do not cook rare, Jews
only cook well done. Originally the reasons for this were explained
by the rules of the kosher kitchen, but even if you don't keep
kosher, and, by the way, my recipes are not meant to conform to
a strictly kosher kitchen (though they can be adapted to do so), to
me it still makes sense to cook things well done to kill the bacteria
and who knows what else. Remember what Mama always says,
you don't know where it's been or for how long.

With Jewish food you know what you're eating—it's simple and it's tasty and most of all there's plenty of it. In a nutshell, Jewish food is food that makes people happy.

"Do you have a philosophy of cooking, Mama?" is another question that people like to ask me, particularly on television and radio. Well, I certainly do, and I think that most of you will be glad to hear it. I believe in delicious food that is simple and easy to make. I believe you should never make three pots dirty, when one will do. Some of you may be shocked when you read some of my recipes to find that I have eliminated many steps that we have been told by the expert cooks are essential. But I appeal to common sense. If, for example, you're making a stew that's going to cook for several hours anyway, there is no point in browning the meat first to seal in the juices or whatever. The meat is going to get cooked, and, believe me, it's going to be delicious. Trust me.

Another thing: you will notice in the list of ingredients that follow that I tend to use certain prepared foods in my cooking. Oi, shocking! But I'm not making excuses, because, again, it's just common sense: If somebody makes a good thing, what should we do, pretend it's no good? There is no better mayonnaise than Hellman's and that's what I use, always. Heinz makes the best ketchup, and a cup or two for flavoring are indispensable in many of my recipes. And, to tell you the truth, my meat loaf, which more than one total stranger has called the best meat loaf in the world, cannot be made without Campbell's tomato soup.

So finally, *kinderlach*, we get to the question: "Mama, who is this book for?" I'm looking you straight in the eye and I'm telling you this: "It's for everyone." All right, maybe very, very experienced cooks may think (only at first) that it's too simple. But still, I tell you: this is how your own mother and grandmother cooked—you need to hold on to that, to remember. And you need to remember that not everything has to be complicated in order to be tasty and satisfying.

If you're a beginning cook, this book is for you because nothing is complicated and everything is easy to learn. Right from the start, you can make delicious meals. If you're a busy careerperson, this book is for you because you can find recipes that are made quickly and other recipes that can be made way ahead of time. Remember, if you're going to work like a *meshuggeneh* (crazy person), you need nourishment! If you're a prince or a princess, this book will encourage you to get off your *tuchis* once in a while and get into the kitchen and do your share. You'll find it very rewarding. If you're cooking for a large family or like to entertain your friends, most of my recipes can be made in large quantities ahead of time, and most of the food in this book only gets better with reheating.

Finally a word about quantities. My amounts for what people eat are based on old-time Jewish portions—when hungry people didn't know or care about calories. So the final number of portions that any recipe yields depends on whether the people you are feeding are *fressers* (big eaters) or weight watchers.

Enough now. About me, that is. It's time to get into the kitchen and start cooking . . . Mama Leah style!

# INGREDIENTS IN MAMA LEAH'S KITCHEN

*The Kosher Kitchen.*  This is not intended to be a kosher cookbook, but for all my readers who keep a kosher home and follow the laws of *kashrut,* you will note that I do not include any ingredients that are considered "trayfe," such as pork, shellfish, etc. Many of the recipes can be made kosher or parve by substituting margarine or corn oil where butter is used.

In case you don't know about kosher food, here's a very simplified explanation. Jewish people divide food into four basic categories. These are:

1. Milchig. These are all dairy foods, which include milk, cream, butter, and cheese. These foods are never served or eaten together with the fleischig foods (meats) from the following category.
2. Flaischig. These are all meats and poultry that are not consid-

ered trayfe (forbidden). Flaischig foods are never eaten together with milchig foods.

3. Parve. These are considered neutral foods that are neither
meat nor dairy. They include vegetables, fruits, fish, and eggs.
These foods can be eaten together with either milchig or flaischig foods.

4. Trayfe. These are strictly forbidden to be eaten at any time.
Trayfe foods include pork, shellfish, or the blood of any animal.

*The Kosher Butcher Shop.* My mother, though
she didn't keep a strictly kosher home, insisted on buying only
kosher meats and poultry. "Kosher" translates loosely to mean
"clean" or "pure" and means that the laws of *kashrut* have been
strictly observed. Many types of meat such as pork are not permitted at all. With other animals, only certain cuts of meat are considered kosher. Under the laws of *kashrut,* only meat from animals
that are ritually slaughtered in a specific way to be the least painful
to the animal, and to rid the carcass of as much blood as possible,
is used. The blood of any animal or fowl is considered trayfe, or
forbidden. That is why Jews never eat their meat rare or pink. The
slaughtering is always done by a qualified person called a *schochet.*

Even though kosher meats and poultry already have had a lot of
blood removed in the butchering process, my mother always did
her own kashering at home on all meat and poultry before cooking
it. This involved smearing the meat or poultry with kosher salt,
letting it sit for half an hour on a draining board, and then washing
it thoroughly under cold running water.

*The Fish Market.* If you are lucky enough to live in a
town that has a fresh-fish market, it is well worth your while to be
on good terms with the people who run it. A friendly fishmonger
can teach you a lot about what to look for in a fresh fish and can
also be prevailed upon to order varieties of fish he doesn't normally carry.

*Whitefish.* Unfortunately this delicious freshwater fish is
not at all commonly found in fish markets in the Northeast. You

will probably have to ask your fishmonger to order it for you, but be sure to stress that you want the freshwater variety, as it is sometimes confused with a saltwater fish that is not at all a suitable substitute. I believe it is much more readily available in parts of the Midwest and the Northwest. My niece, Debbie, who lives in Montana, says whitefish is always available in local markets because of the many lakes in the area. Whitefish is the only fish I use to make gefilte fish.

*S m e l t s .*    These small, delicious fish are not as readily available as they once were, perhaps because most people don't seem to know what to do with them. This is a shame because smelts are some of the most delectable of all fishes and even people who normally don't like fish can't get over the delicious flavor of my fried smelts. I read in A. J. McClane's *Encyclopedia of Fish Cookery* that smelts were once so abundant in the Back Bay of Boston that "distinguished merchants of lower Beacon Street might be seen, at early hours, eagerly catching their breakfast from their back doors."

Although fresh smelts are incomparably good, smelts do freeze amazingly well and should you find them frozen in your market don't hesitate to bring them home and fry them. On the other hand, in the spring, when smelts are running, it would certainly be worth your while to *hok* (nag) your fishmonger into ordering the freshest smelts he can get hold of.

If you've never eaten smelts before, then I will tell you that the bones in this fish are so soft you can eat the whole thing. Some people even eat the heads. I don't, but some do.

*The Appetizing Store.*    Anybody who grew up in New York City is well acquainted with the appetizing store as a place you went to get lox, Nova, herring of every sort, pickles, salads, breads, cream cheese with scallions, and endless other scrumptious goodies. There are not so many of these neighborhood stores left anymore—although there are the grand emporiums like Zabar's on Manhattan's Upper West Side, and there are still wonderful specialty stores like Russ and Daughters on the Lower East Side. But for most people the appetizing store has shrunk down to a small corner of a supermarket.

*Herring.*   Most of the herring we can buy today comes from Canada and is caught in North Atlantic waters. All the different kinds of herring you see in the appetizing department start off as herring that has been cured by salting. So the most basic kind of herring is a salt herring, and salt herrings are used to make all the other kinds of herring. Schmaltz herring is a salt herring that has been prepared in a "fancy," that is to say, "schmaltzy," way. "Schmaltz" means "fat" in Yiddish, but it also means "fancy." All herrings are fatty fish, and in this instance you have a herring that is both fat and fancy because it is served marinated in oil and with slices of onion. Pickled herring is a salt herring that has been pickled. Matjes herring is a salt herring that has been marinated in wine and aged in sandalwood casks.

*Lox and Nova.*   What's the difference between lox and Nova? Both are types of salmon and by me both are delicious. Also, both are relatively recent additions to Jewish cuisine. Our word "lox" comes from the Scandinavian *lax* and the German *lachs,* both of which are words that just mean salmon. When you buy lox today it generally comes from the Pacific Ocean, and the name implies that it has been cured by soaking in salt but not by smoking. It's considered inferior to Nova, and so the price is lower, but there are those who prefer it for its own sake because they love the saltier, tangier taste of lox. Nova, on the other hand, is made from fish caught in eastern or Atlantic waters, and it's salted and smoked, and it's pretty expensive.

*Eggs.*   Today eggs are mass produced and often stored so long on the refrigerator shelves that by the time you eat them they have very little flavor and no freshness whatsoever. If you can find a source of freshly laid eggs, try them, because you will be amazed at the difference in taste. Many health food stores sell eggs that are from free range chickens (a varied diet for the hen produces tastier eggs) and are considerably fresher than supermarket eggs.

*Hard-boiled Eggs.*   Everybody should know how to boil an egg.

# How to Make Hard-Boiled Eggs

*Eggs*                                    *½ tablespoon kosher salt*
*Water*                                   *¼ cup white vinegar*

Place eggs in a saucepan and cover the eggs with cold water by at
least 2 inches. Add the kosher salt and white vinegar. Bring to a
boil, reduce heat to a simmer, and cook for 25 to 30 minutes. Drain
and let cold water run over the eggs while you tap each egg lightly
with a spoon to just crack it. Let the eggs sit in cold water until they
have cooled completely. This will make it easy for you to peel
them. The center of the yolks should be very hard and have a
slightly milky color.

*S c h m a l t z   a n d   G r i e b e n .*   Schmaltz, the rendered fat
from a chicken or goose, was to the Jews of Europe what olive oil
is to the Mediterranean peoples. Oil of any kind was rare and
expensive, and being poor and thrifty forced the homemaker to
find a readily available substitute. So schmaltz it was, and back in
the days when people naturally burned more calories and knew
less about the causes of heart disease, the word "schmaltz" was
equivalent to wealth and riches. How could anything so delicious
be bad for you?

   Today, of course, we know better. But, still, loaded with cholesterol though it is, the flavor of rendered chicken fat in cooking is
like ambrosia. I've called for it in some recipes (though you are,
of course, always free to substitute corn oil) because I feel that
everyone should once in a while get to taste the real thing.

   Here's how to make it:

# Schmaltz

Remove as much fat as possible, along with some of the skin, from chickens before cooking them. Cut the chicken fat and skin into small pieces. Save the fat in plastic bags in the freezer until you have 3 to 4 cups of chicken fat and skins and you are ready to render it.

Place 3 to 4 cups raw chicken fat and skins in a large, heavy skillet or frying pan. Cook over moderate heat until the fat liquefies and the solid pieces become much smaller and turn golden brown. Add a medium onion that you have chopped up into small pieces. When the onion and the skins have become crisp and very brown, remove from heat. Remove the crispy skins with a slotted spoon (these are the grieben) and add them to chopped liver or serve them for a very fattening but delicious snack. Add 1 teaspoon salt to the rendered chicken fat, stir, and let stand until slightly cooled but still liquid. You should have about 1 cup of schmaltz. Pour into a glass jar and refrigerate or freeze. Schmaltz will last indefinitely either way.

*Grieben.* You can keep the grieben covered in the refrigerator and reheat them in a slow oven (300°F) until they are crispy, before serving.

*B u t t e r .*  When I use butter it is always the sweet or unsalted variety. If you are watching your cholesterol, you can substitute margarine everywhere butter is called for.

*C l a r i f i e d  B u t t e r .*  When butter has been clarified it means that all the casein and other sediments have been removed. You can use clarified butter to cook foods at higher temperatures without the butter turning brown and burnt tasting. This is particularly good for frying blintzes. If you go to the trouble of making clarified butter, you will be rewarded by the fact that it keeps in the refrigerator indefinitely, so you can keep it on hand until it's time to make more. Even without refrigeration, clarified butter will keep for a long time without getting rancid.

*To make clarified butter.* Melt a quantity of butter in a saucepan over low heat. When the butter has melted completely cook for a few minutes longer until all the milk solids have settled to the bottom of the pan. Skim away any foam that has formed on the surface of the butter. Remove from heat, let stand for 5 minutes, then carefully pour off the clear butter into a clean container. Discard the milky solids on the bottom.

*O i l .*  I use corn oil almost exclusively, but you can substitute safflower or sunflower oil if you like. I don't use olive oil for cooking but save it for special salad dressings.

*M a y o n n a i s e .*  I would never bother to make my own mayonnaise as long as Hellmann's was available. Now, I also use Hellmann's Light and Hellmann's Cholesterol Free Reduced Calorie Mayonnaise. These are not quite as tasty as the regular but if you're watching your fat and calorie intake, they make a very good substitute. If you live west of the Rockies, Hellmann's is called Best Foods Mayonnaise.

## *Mama Leah's Pantry*

*W h i t e   R i c e .*  I almost always use Uncle Ben's.

*B r o w n   R i c e .*  Any brown rice is good. I prefer a short-grain brown rice because it has a nice nutty flavor. You may have to go to the health food store to find short-grain brown rice. If they make a distinction between "organic" brown rice and regular brown rice, get the regular, which I find to be more uniform in size and cleaner. I have often had a feeling that the so-called "organic" brown rice is inferior rice passed off as organic. All brown rice should be washed in several changes of cool water, until the water runs clear and clean.

*B a r l e y .*  I use pearl barley from the grocery story. I know there are other kinds of barley sold in health food stores, but I have never tried them. Just remember one thing about barley—it expands like crazy when you cook it and even after you cook it, so that if you make a soup or a stew with barley in it and leave it in the refrigerator for the next day, you will probably need to add some more liquid when you reheat. A friend of mine told me that at Jewish weddings in Hungary they used to throw barley at the bride and groom to encourage fertility.

*K a s h a .*    Kasha is the name given to roasted buckwheat groats. You can find it on supermarket shelves sold under the Wolff's label. It comes in several sizes: fine, medium, coarse, and whole. Any of these can be used, but I prefer the medium, with coarse as second choice. You can also find kasha in health food stores under the Pocono label. Here, too, you might find pale unroasted buckwheat groats, which I'm told are very good but don't have the rich, nutty flavor of the dark roasted kasha groats.

Even people who know and love kasha are surprised to discover that buckwheat groats are not a grain at all but fruit related botanically more to rhubarb than to wheat. It is a plant that prospers in climates and areas where growing wheat is not possible. It is very nutritious because it is high in protein, B vitamins, iron, and calcium, and it is a perfect grain substitute for people who have allergies to wheat.

*V a r n i s h k e s .*    These are bowtie-shaped egg noodles, usually made by Goodman's. Other macaroni bowties may be substituted, even *farfalle,* which are Italian bowtie noodles. If you can't find any bowtie noodles, you can still substitute wide egg noodles broken into pieces 2½ to 3 inches long.

*E g g   B a r l e y   o r   F a r f e l .*    Farfel is made from egg noodle dough that is cut into little bits and then toasted to give it a rich, nutty flavor. If you have never had it, try it, it could be the beginning of a love affair. Goodman's is the best, make sure it says "toasted" on the box. If you can't find "toasted" egg barley, you can toast it yourself. Preheat your oven to 350°F. Spread the farfel on a foil-lined cookie sheet and bake in the oven for 15 to 20 minutes, stirring it around from time to time so it toasts evenly.

*Chick-peas.*   These beans have been around for a long, long time. They're called *ceci* in Italian, and someone told me that Cicero's name is derived from this bean. You can use canned chick-peas in almost all the recipes except for making Abbas (page 37). For this, you must start from scratch with dried chick-peas. These must be soaked overnight before cooking them. When I have time to soak and cook the chick-peas, I prefer the dried chick-peas to the canned in all my recipes because they have a better flavor and texture. In case you don't know it, chick-peas are very good for you—high in protein, calcium, iron, and B vitamins. If your supermarket doesn't carry dried chick-peas, look in a health food store or in Italian, Spanish, Greek, or Middle Eastern grocery stores.

*Lima Beans.*   Many kinds of canned beans are very good and I use them when I don't have time to soak and cook the dried kind. Lima beans are different. Canned, they're terrible. Don't even bother. So most of the lima beans called for in my recipes are the dried kind, either the big ones or the baby ones. They taste the same, but the little ones cook a little quicker. Occasionally I will use frozen lima beans in a casserole or as a vegetable on their own, but most of the time dried lima beans are the kind I'm talking about. They need to be soaked, and if you have the patience, it's good to rub the soaking beans between your fingers and remove the skins. Sometimes I do, sometimes I don't. You may be interested to know that lima beans came from Peru (remember Lima, as in the capital of Peru?) and date back at least seventy-five hundred years, but how they left the Americas and showed up in shtetls in Eastern Europe is an unsolved mystery.

*Split Peas.*   Dried split peas come in green and yellow. The yellow variety is very popular among Scandinavians, and I knew a Swedish family who had yellow split pea soup every Thursday night without fail. I love split pea soup and could even eat it once a week, but, as it happens, I prefer the green split peas. Whichever variety you prefer, you don't need to soak them. They are easy to cook, economical, and nutritionally very good for you. So maybe split pea soup once a week isn't such a bad idea?

*Lentils.*   Lentils are thought to be the oldest cultivated legume, and some people date it from about 8000 B.C. As you probably know from reading the Old Testament, Esau sold his birthright for a dish of stewed lentils, and lentils have fed the hungry of this world ever since. There have been times when lentils have lost some of their popularity because they came to be associated with poor people's food, but today they are making a comeback and you find them being served in even very fancy restaurants. And no wonder, they're delicious, high in protein, totally lacking in fat, and have lots of minerals and vitamins.

Lentils come in a variety of sizes and colors—brown, green, and red—and although I use the regular brown lentils found on the supermarket shelves, you can substitute any of the others in recipes if you want to experiment. All lentils should be picked over very carefully to remove any small stones and grit and washed in several changes of cold water. There is no need to soak them before cooking.

*Flour.*   I use Heckers unbleached all-purpose flour for all my baking. If you live in the Midwest, the same flour is called Ceresota.

*Matzo.*   This is an unleavened square cracker that is eaten instead of other bread during Passover. It is available in almost all supermarkets year round, and I prefer to use it in place of any other kinds of biscuits or crackers. You may prefer to switch to matzos as well when you realize that they are made without any animal or saturated fats of any kind. Most other crackers tend to be loaded with fats, especially palm and coconut oil, which are both high in saturated fat.

*Matzo Meal.*   Like bread crumbs, only made from matzos. Great used for any breading or stuffing.

*Matzo Cake Meal.*   This is finely ground matzo and is used instead of flour during Passover.

*C o r n m e a l .*  The cornmeal available in supermarkets is perfectly adequate, but you will get a better flavor from stone-ground cornmeal bought in the health food store or by mail order from the mill itself. Stone-ground cornmeal is not degerminated and therefore has more vitamins and taste. Because the germ of the corn has not been removed, it can become rancid unless it is kept refrigerated. Cornmeal comes white or yellow, depending on the type of corn it was made from. I prefer the yellow because that's the one I'm used to, but you can use either one.

Two sources of excellent stone-ground cornmeal are:

> Morgan's Mills
> RD 2
> Box 115
> Union, Maine 04862
> Telephone: (207) 785-4900

> and

> Kenyon Cornmeal Company
> Usquepaugh, Rhode Island 02892
> Telephone: (401) 783-4054

*B o u i l l o n   C u b e s   a n d   P o w d e r s .*  I like to use Knorr bouillon cubes, and they're so good that I use them a lot. I use them to make broth and to season a weak broth that needs more flavor. They come in four flavors—beef, chicken, fish, and vegetarian. I keep all four on hand.

I also use MBT instant broth (chicken and beef) when a quick-dissolving powder is useful rather than a slow-dissolving cube.

*C h r a i n   ( H o r s e r a d i s h ) .*  Sholom Aleichem's great character, Tevye, the milkman, says that "Horseradish that doesn't bring a pious tear to the eye is not God's horseradish." In the old days every housewife made her own horseradish sauce from fresh horseradish root, which was grated and mixed with salt, sugar, and vinegar, and sometimes with a grated beet to give it a lovely red color. And every housewife knew that grating horseradish root, like chopping onions, was likely to bring a tear or two to the eyes. Today we can buy prepared horseradish in jars (found re-frigerated in your supermarket) and it is very good indeed. So there's no need to cry. Unless, of course, you happen to take a big mouthful. But it's good for you and clears the sinuses.

If you would like to try making it from scratch, here's how:

# Chrain (Grated Horseradish)

*1 fresh horseradish root, 3 to 4 inches long*
*4 tablespoons vinegar (plain white or cider)*
*2 teaspoons salt*
*1 teaspoon sugar*
*2 cooked and peeled beets (canned are okay), optional*

Peel the horseradish root and grate it by hand using a grater, or use the shredding disk on a food processor. Some people love it freshly grated with nothing else added. But if you want to keep it for any length of time, put it in a bowl, add the vinegar and salt, and mix well. Now you have white horseradish. If you want the red variety, grate or shred the beets and stir them into the horseradish. Horseradish will keep very well in the refrigerator if you store it in a tightly covered jar.

*Garlic.*   The ancient Hebrews believed that garlic was one of the most potent aphrodisiacs available. Maybe that's why we sur-vived for thousands of years. It was also thought to ward off sick-ness when hung around the neck. It might work, who would go near you? But actually, now we know that garlic is good for you—doctors and scientists say so. What I do know for sure is that life without garlic would be very bland indeed.

In my recipes, when I call for garlic to be crushed, I mean pushed through a garlic press.

*Garlic Powder.*  I use unsalted garlic powder in some of my recipes because it adds a nice, strong flavor. But it is not a good substitute for fresh garlic.

*Ketchup.*  Ketchup is called for in a number of my recipes, and before you start to look down your nose at this let me tell you that this is a trick I learned from a fabulous cook in France. This was a lady whose ragouts, potages, and pâtés were so good they could make you swoon. When I asked her what her secret was, she smiled a shy, sly smile, opened her cupboard and pulled out a bottle of ketchup. She was convinced that ketchup was America's most important contribution to the culinary arts. Heinz ketchup is the brand I use.

*Salt.*  When salt is called for in these recipes I mean kosher salt. Kosher salt is widely available in supermarkets and I happen to like its large-grained, coarse texture. It has no additives like iodine or fillers like cornstarch, which is added to regular table salt to make it pour more smoothly.

*Sauerkraut.*  The best sauerkraut comes fresh from a barrel and can be found in good delicatessens. Otherwise, canned sauerkraut is also very good. Third best is the kind that comes packaged in plastic and can be found in the refrigerated section of your supermarket.

   I once watched a friend make her own sauerkraut, and let me tell you, I did not think it was worth the bother. It takes so much time and effort and the store-bought sauerkraut is really just as good.

## Herbs and Spices

*Dill.*  Dill is delicious fresh but not very good dried. Luckily, though, it freezes perfectly. Chop it up fine and wrap in tinfoil. It defrosts quickly and can be substituted for fresh anytime. I've always got some stowed away in my freezer.

*P a r s l e y .*  I use Italian flat-leafed parsley for flavoring and cooking and curly-leafed parsley for decoration. Parsley does not freeze or dry well, but you can usually find it in the supermarket.

*B a y  L e a v e s .*  These are used in soups and stews. The most flavorful are imported from Europe. They are used to impart flavor and aroma but are not themselves edible and should be removed from the finished dish before serving.

*C i n n a m o n .*  Cinnamon adds a sweet, spicy taste to fruits and baked goods.

*C l o v e s .*  I use whole, not powdered cloves. I try to remember to remove them from the finished dish because if you bite into a whole clove, you will think that you have been to the dentist.

*O r e g a n o .*  I don't use this Italian herb very often, but when I do, I love it.

*T h y m e .*  Dried thyme is delicious in soups, gravies, and stuffings.

# 1

# APPETIZERS

□ □ □ □ □ □ □ □ □ □ □ □ □ □ □ □ □ □ □ □ □ □ □ □ □ □ □ □ □ □

I *have often thought* that the word "appetizer" looks and
sounds like a contraction of the words "appetite" and "teaser."
And that is exactly what appetizers are supposed to do—tease your
appetite—bring your taste buds along to a full, quivering appreciation of the main course. In Yiddish, we call appetizers the "forspeis," which means the foretaste of what's to come. All this is well
and good, but I myself am sure that the idea of appetizers, back in
the old country, originally came about to do just the opposite—you
put out an appetizer or two to fill up the hungry bellies and stretch
the main entrée to more or less feed everybody who needed to be
fed. Many appetizers were made up of little bits and pieces of
leftovers to begin with. But a good cook knows how to turn a
hard-boiled egg and a piece of herring into a tasty tidbit.

Today everybody I know loves appetizers. Appetizers set the
mood. They say to your family and guests, "At this meal we are not
just going to stuff our faces, we're going to experience a variety of

tastes and textures—we are going to feed our senses as well as our bellies." Appetizers don't have to be fancy, but they should always be presented in a way that looks nice and pleases the eye. And, remember, sometimes the best meal you can make is to put together a nice assortment of appetizers and forget the main course. Everyone will admire your originality and your chutzpah!

A lot of the appetizers found in this chapter can be put together to make a great brunch or Sunday-morning breakfast. In which case I guess they become an appetizer for the rest of the day.

Whether you call them appetizers in English, forspeis in Yiddish, zakuski in Russian, hors d'oeuvres in French, meze in Greek, tapas in Spanish, and antipasto in Italian—everybody has 'em and everybody loves 'em.

## Pickled Herring

My father may not have been a great provider, but he was a great pickled herring maker. I used to walk the two miles with him while he carried a large panful of his pickled herring over to my Aunt Bessie and Uncle Moishe's home. The proud and happy look on his face when he presented his gift to them is unforgettable to me. His herring was always gratefully received and happily eaten. This is his recipe and I'm proud to pass it on.

| | |
|---|---|
| *6 salt herring fillets* | *2 tablespoons sugar* |
| *4 large onions, thinly sliced* | *1 tablespoon pickling spice* |
| *1 cup white vinegar* | *4 bay leaves* |
| *½ cup water* | |

Wash the herring fillets well under cold running water and place them in a glass or crockery bowl. Cover with cold water and refrigerate overnight (about 10 to 12 hours).

Rinse herrings again and place them in a glass or enameled

casserole or baking pan. Cover with sliced onions, making layers if necessary.

Now make the marinade. In a saucepan combine vinegar, water, sugar, pickling spice, and bay leaves. Bring to a boil and reduce to a simmer. Cook for 3 to 5 minutes until sugar is dissolved. Cool slightly and pour over the herring. Cover and place in a cool spot or refrigerate and marinate for 2 to 3 days before serving. Remove the herring fillets from the marinade and slice into bite-size pieces. Place in a serving bowl, mix with marinade and onions, and serve.

YIELD: *10 to 12 servings.*

*Advice from Mama:* While my father used an old-fashioned enameled pan in which to soak and marinate the herring, I prefer to use those nice plastic containers that come in different shapes and sizes, each with its own lid. They're manufactured by Rubbermaid and sold in grocery stores and hardware stores. Sometimes progress is great.

# Herring in Cream Sauce

> The child was ushered into the world with an array of herring. A Briss meant HERRING. For months before the great day our house was inhabited by pickled herrings. Jars, big ones, little ones, glass and clay ones. Eyes, herring eyes, staring at you through windows, in clothing closets, on fire escapes—the phosphorescent glow of herrings swinging on onion hoops.
> —*Sam Levenson*

You can buy herring in cream sauce already made in delis, specialty stores, and even in jars in the supermarket. Some of the ones I've tried are not bad. But trust me on this—no herring in cream sauce will ever be as good as the one you make yourself, from my recipe, of course. The only thing you need to do is plan ahead because the herring takes time to soak and marinate. So be sure you start 3 or 4 days before you plan to serve. Otherwise the preparation couldn't be easier.

| | |
|---|---|
| *6 salt herring fillets* | *2 tablespoons sugar* |
| *4 large onions, thinly sliced* | *1 tablespoon pickling spice* |
| *1 cup white vinegar* | *4 bay leaves* |
| *½ cup water* | *1 cup sour cream* |

Wash the herring fillets well under cold running water and place them in a glass or crockery bowl. Cover with cold water and refrigerate overnight (about 10 to 12 hours).

Rinse herrings again and place them in a glass or enameled casserole or baking pan. Cover with sliced onions, making layers if necessary.

Now make the marinade. In a saucepan combine vinegar, water, sugar, pickling spice, and bay leaves. Bring to a boil and reduce to a simmer. Cook for 3 to 5 minutes until sugar is dissolved. Remove from heat and allow to cool. Combine sour cream with the cooled marinade and pour over the herring. Cover and refrigerate for 2 to 3 days before serving. Just before serving, remove the herring fillets from marinade and slice into bite-size pieces. Place in a serving bowl, mix with onions and marinade, and serve.

YIELD:  *10 to 12 servings.*

*Advice from Mama:*  Don't use metal pans (particularly aluminum) for soaking or preparing herring because the salt in the herring can pit or corrode the metal. Stainless steel is probably okay, but glass, crockery, or enamelware is best.

# Chopped Herring

I wonder if the American Medical Association ever heard the old saying from a Polish rabbi, "In a place where they eat a lot of herring, they don't need a lot of doctors." Here's one of my favorite ways to enjoy herring.

| | |
|---|---|
| *2 pickled herring fillets* | *2 hard-boiled eggs, peeled* |
| *2 slices white bread or challah,* | *1 small onion, coarsely diced* |
| *crusts removed* | *2 tablespoons corn oil* |
| *3 tablespoons white vinegar* | *Pinch of freshly ground black* |
| *or* | *pepper* |
| *Juice of 1 lemon* | *1 teaspoon sugar or to taste* |
| *1 large tart apple (Granny Smith* | |
| *preferred)* | |

Cut the herring fillets into ½-inch pieces and remove any skin and bones you find. Tear or cut the bread into small pieces and soak in vinegar or lemon juice. Peel and core the apple and cut into eighths.

Place all the ingredients, except sugar, in the bowl of a food processor. Process a few seconds to a fairly smooth pulp. Taste to see if you think sugar is necessary to cut the sharpness. Arrange in a serving bowl and refrigerate until ready to serve. Serve with Bagel Chips or Rye Garlic Toasts (both on page 42).

YIELD: *4 to 6 servings.*

*Advice from Mama:* If you don't have a store that sells herring fillets in your neighborhood, you can substitute a 1-pint jar of herring in wine sauce from your supermarket.

Another variation of this recipe is to use salt herring fillets (also known as schmaltz herring) instead of pickled herring. You should soak the herring fillets in cold water to cover overnight (about 10 to 12 hours), changing the water twice. Rinse well under cold running water, dry on paper towels, and proceed with the recipe above.

# Herring Salad

In the fictional village of Chelm people believed that the waters of the ocean were becoming saltier every day because of all the herrings living there. They worried that the same thing would happen to the lakes and rivers. So much salt must be bad, said the Wise Men of Chelm, so it became everybody's responsibility to eat as much herring as possible. Why else would Jews eat so much herring?

One of my favorite ways to eat herring is in this scrumptious herring salad.

*2 pickled herring fillets*
*2 large boiled potatoes*
*1 medium onion, finely chopped*
*1 small dill pickle, finely chopped*
*1 cup cooked beets (canned are fine), finely chopped*
*1 large apple, peeled, cored, and diced (optional)*
*1/2 cup chopped celery*
*2 tablespoons fresh lemon juice*
*or*
*2 tablespoons wine vinegar*
*1/2 cup sour cream or plain yogurt*
*Freshly ground black pepper*

Cut the herring fillets into 1/2-inch strips. Peel the boiled potatoes and cut into 1/2-inch cubes. Place the herring, potatoes, onion, pickle, beets, apple, and celery in a large mixing bowl. Mix together the lemon juice or vinegar with the sour cream or yogurt. Stir in freshly ground black pepper. Combine with salad ingredients in bowl and mix well.

Y I E L D :   *4 servings.*

*Advice from Mama:*   This makes a very nice starter for a meal. It can be prepared way ahead of time so there is no last minute fussing. You can make it pretty by serving the salad on top of leaves from a head of Boston lettuce.

# Pickled Salmon

My brother-in-law George adores my pickled salmon. He constantly says to me, "Leah, when are you going to make some of your pickled salmon?" So now I can say to him, "Here, George, here's my recipe. You can make it yourself."

*3 medium onions, sliced*
*2 teaspoons salt*
*½ teaspoon white pepper*
*2 cups cold water*
*6 salmon steaks*

*½ cup white vinegar*
*1 tablespoon sugar*
*1½ teaspoons pickling spice*
*5 whole peppercorns*
*1 bay leaf*

In a large saucepan combine 1 sliced onion, salt, white pepper, and the cold water. Bring to a boil and reduce to a simmer. Gently slide in the salmon steaks and simmer for 15 to 20 minutes, until fish is done.

Spread half the remaining sliced onions in a glass or ceramic dish. Remove the salmon steaks from the poaching liquid (but save the liquid) and place on top of the onions and cover with remaining sliced onions.

To the poaching liquid in the saucepan add the vinegar, sugar, pickling spice, peppercorns, and bay leaf. Bring to a boil, reduce heat to a simmer, and cook for 5 minutes. Strain the stock and pour over the fish. Allow to cool completely, cover and refrigerate for 2 days. Serve cold as an appetizer or lunch dish. Pickled salmon will keep well, refrigerated, for up to a week.

Y I E L D :   *4 to 6 servings, 12 servings as an appetizer.*

*Advice from Mama:*   Pickled whitefish makes a nice alternative to pickled salmon and some people, like my sister Shirley, who only likes her salmon broiled or poached, prefer it. Substitute 1 large whitefish, cleaned and cut into 6 to 8 steaks, in the above recipe.

# Cream Cheese and Nova Spread

Here's a really easy recipe that can change an ordinary breakfast of coffee and bagels into a special brunch. I prefer the more delicate flavor of Nova Scotia smoked salmon for this dish, but many people like the more assertive taste of lox. You decide for yourself.

*1 pound cream cheese*
*¼ pound Nova Scotia smoked*
  *salmon or lox*

Place cream cheese in mixing bowl and leave at room temperature until soft. Dice the Nova or lox into very small pieces. Blend with an electric beater until well mixed and fluffy. Refrigerate and serve cold as a spread.

If you wish, you may dress this up by shaping it in a pretty mold. Line a small mold with plastic wrap, pack the cream cheese into the mold on top of plastic wrap. Cover and refrigerate for several hours or overnight. To serve, invert the mold, with the top unwrapped, onto a serving plate. Remove the mold and then carefully peel away the plastic wrap.

Serve with cocktail-size rounds of pumpernickel and rye bread or mini bagels if available. Or have with regular toasted bagels for brunch.

YIELD: *Enough for 8 to 10 servings.*

*Advice from Mama:* You can add some finely chopped scallions and/or a little snipped fresh dill to gussy this up for a fancy cocktail party.

# Cream Cheese and Caviar Roll

This is a great fancy-looking appetizer to make with inexpensive caviar. Don't use beluga even if you can afford it. It would be a waste. If you need help eating it, just call me up.

*1 pound cream cheese*
*2 to 3 ounces black or red*
*   caviar*

Soften cream cheese to room temperature. Line a cookie sheet with waxed paper, then spread cream cheese on waxed paper into a large rectangle. Using a spatula, spread the caviar on the cream cheese, reserving a small amount for garnishing. Refrigerate for about 10 minutes, or until cream cheese starts to firm up. Roll the cream cheese like a jelly roll, pulling the waxed paper away as you shape the roll. Garnish the top of the roll with reserved caviar and refrigerate until firm. Trim the sides with a knife dipped in hot water.

Serve with crackers or bagel crisps.

YIELD: *1 cream cheese caviar roll, for about 16 to 20 servings, depending on what other appetizers there are.*

*Advice from Mama:* This is a great appetizer for a party. To make it look even more festive, serve it on a bed of chopped watercress and coarsely chopped red onion. The watercress and onion are particularly tasty with the cream cheese and caviar.

# Cream Cheese and Scallions

A lot of delis serve their own already made-up mixtures of cream cheese and scallions, but to me it always tastes as if it's been sitting around too long. The best thing about scallions is their taste, so fresh and green, when you first slice them up into the thinnest possible rounds. Anyway, where could you find an easier recipe? In case you come from Mars, cream cheese and scallions is a classic of the brunch table. But it is also good as a snack or appetizer on a cracker or a piece of rye bread.

*1 pound cream cheese*
*4 to 5 scallions, trimmed and*
  *diced fine, green part included*

Place cream cheese in mixing bowl and leave at room temperature until soft. Add scallions and blend with an electric beater until well mixed and fluffy. Refrigerate and serve cold as a spread.

If you wish, you may dress this up by shaping it in a pretty mold. Line a small mold with plastic wrap, pack the cream cheese into the mold on top of plastic wrap. Cover and refrigerate for several hours or overnight. To serve, invert the mold, with the top unwrapped, onto a serving plate. Remove the mold and then carefully peel away the plastic wrap.

Serve with bagels, your favorite crackers, or bread.

YIELD: *8 to 10 servings as a spread for bagels, more if served as an appetizer.*

*Advice from Mama:* You can make the cream cheese mold look even more festive by surrounding it with slices of tomatoes and sprigs of fresh dill.


# Creamy Egg Salad

Okay, you love egg salad as much as I do. Who doesn't? But you're worried about cholesterol. Here's what to do. Be good all week, eat lots of brown rice, kasha, and steamed vegetables. Get plenty of exercise—walk, dance, jump rope, ride a bike—and once a week Doctor Mama Leah says you can have a little egg salad. Put it on whole wheat bread. *Mmmm.* Now get off your *tuchis* (what you're sitting on) and take a brisk walk.

| | |
|---|---|
| *12 hard-boiled eggs, peeled* | *Pinch of white pepper* |
| *5 tablespoons Hellmann's* | |
| *mayonnaise* | |

Cut the eggs into large chunks. Add mayonnaise and pepper and mix well. If you prefer egg salad a little drier, add less mayo and vice versa. Serve on lettuce-lined plates or as a sandwich spread.

YIELD: *4 salads or 6 thick sandwiches.*

*Advice from Mama:* When it comes to egg salad I'm a purist and I never add anything else. Not even salt, because the mayonnaise gives it enough seasoning. If you're a "saltaholic," put some in, but, remember, it's not healthy. If you feel you must be experimental and add something else, you can choose from a little bit of very finely diced celery, finely diced scallion, and finely chopped dill. That's it. Now go take that walk.

# Chopped Egg and Onion

Another classic from my mother's kitchen. Who would think that such simple ingredients could come out so delicious? This makes a perfect appetizer spread for crackers or matzos. It makes a great sandwich with a little lettuce or a slice of tomato, or both.

| | |
|---|---|
| *12 hard-boiled eggs, peeled* | *½ teaspoon salt or to taste* |
| *1 small onion, diced fine* | *Pinch of white pepper (optional)* |
| *⅓ cup Schmaltz (rendered* | |
| *chicken fat) (page 10)* | |

Chop the eggs. You can do this by hand, using a knife and cutting board, or use one of those egg-slicing gadgets or even a half-moon chopper and a wooden bowl. I prefer the eggs chopped fairly small, but you will eventually arrive at your own preference. I've never used a food processor for this because it can so easily turn the eggs into a paste.

Sauté the onion in the schmaltz until it starts to brown. Add to the chopped eggs and mix well. Stir in salt and pepper to taste. Refrigerate until ready to serve. Check seasonings before serving because sometimes cold foods need more salt and pepper.

YIELD: *6 to 8 servings.*

*Advice from Mama:* Sure, you can substitute corn oil (¼ cup) for the rendered chicken fat, but who are you kidding? With 12 eggs, you may as well go ahead and enjoy the great taste of schmaltz. Also, if your schmaltz already has a lot of onion in it, you can leave out the onion in this recipe. But as far as I'm concerned, a little extra onion never hurt.

# Chopped Mushrooms, Egg, and Onion

You'll notice a few "chopped" recipes. These evolved, probably, because they were an easy and inexpensive appetizer, entrée, or sandwich filler. When I was growing up, our sandwich fillings were pretty limited. We couldn't have ham and cheese, there wasn't any kosher bologna (that I know of), tuna and salmon with mayonnaise were considered too expensive for children's sandwiches. And heaven forbid that any Jewish child should be given peanut butter and jelly sandwiches—these treats were strictly for non-Jews. Hence, the "chopped" improvisations.

*1 medium onion, diced fine*
*¼ cup corn oil*
*10 to 12 medium white mushrooms, chopped fine*
*12 hard-boiled eggs, peeled and chopped fine*

*½ teaspoon salt*
*Freshly ground black pepper to taste*

Sauté the onion in corn oil until it starts to turn golden brown. Add the mushrooms and sauté for about 5 minutes, or until mushrooms have softened and turned dark. Stir frequently. Remove from heat and let cool. Mix together with chopped eggs, salt, and pepper. Taste and adjust for seasoning. Refrigerate until ready to use. Serve with pumpernickel, crackers, or melba toast.

YIELD:   *8 to 12 servings.*

*Advice from Mama:*   This is even better if you substitute ⅓ cup Schmaltz (page 10) for the corn oil.

# Chopped Chicken Liver
―――――――――――  ▼  ―――――――――――

There's a whole dispute between the chop-by-hand chicken liver fanatics and the chop-in-a-machine cooks. I've got a machine and I'm always in a hurry, so that's how I make my chopped chicken liver. If you have a lot of time and nothing better to do with it and you'd like to build up your arm muscle, then by all means chop, chop, chop. It'll taste just as good.

*1 pound chicken livers*
*1 large onion, finely chopped*
*¼ cup Schmaltz (rendered*
*   chicken fat) (page 10)*

*3 hard-boiled eggs*
*½ teaspoon salt or to taste*
*Freshly ground black pepper*
*   to taste*

Preheat oven to 375°F.

Wash and drain the chicken livers. Remove all fat and any discolored spots. If you find one with a green area, which is the gall, throw it away. It will make everything taste bitter. Arrange the livers on a foil-lined baking sheet and bake for 30 minutes at 375°F. While livers are baking, sauté the onion in the schmaltz until very brown.

Peel the eggs and chop them coarsely. Place in bowl of food processor or blender. Add the livers, the sautéed onion, salt, and pepper. Pulse the machine until everything is ground and mixed together.

Alternatively, chop everything finely with a half-moon chopping knife in a wooden chopping bowl. Refrigerate until ready to serve.

Serve as an appetizer, on a bed of lettuce with chopped onion.

YIELD: *6 servings.*

*Advice from Mama:*

1. If you're watching your cholesterol, use ⅓ cup corn oil instead of the chicken fat.
2. This makes a great party mold with crackers or rye rounds. For instructions on molding the chopped chicken liver, see recipe for Cream Cheese and Scallions (page 27).
3. To bring out the best flavor, remove from the refrigerator half an hour before serving.

# Chopped Calf's Liver

"Gehakte leber" is the Yiddish for "chopped liver," and when I was growing up, this was the chopped liver we had. Chopped calf's liver has a different taste and texture from chopped chicken liver, slightly more intense in flavor and a little grainier in texture. Chopped chicken liver was hardly ever served because it took much longer to accumulate enough chicken livers to make gehakte leber. Each chicken has only one little liver. Remember that our mothers could only come by a chicken liver when they bought a chicken or two from the kosher butcher. They didn't have freezers and I don't remember any kosher chicken livers being available for sale. Most people of a certain age always prefer chopped calf's liver to the chopped chicken liver, and if they eat chopped chicken liver unknowingly, they are apt to say that the gehakte leber is "a little weak, a little mushy today."

*1 pound calf's liver*
*1 teaspoon salt*
*1 large onion, chopped*
*⅓ to ½ cup Schmaltz (rendered*
*   chicken fat) (page 10) or ⅓*
*   cup corn oil*

*4 hard-boiled eggs*
*Salt and freshly ground black*
*   pepper to taste*

Preheat broiler. Sprinkle liver with salt and broil 3 to 4 minutes on each side, until well done. Sauté the onion in the schmaltz until browned.

Place liver, schmaltz and onions, and hard-boiled eggs in bowl of food processor and grind to smooth consistency. Alternately, grind the liver and the eggs through the medium blade of a food mill or chop finely by hand. Mash together with schmaltz and onions. Season to taste and refrigerate until ready to serve.

Y I E L D :   *6 to 8 servings as an appetizer.*

*Advice from Mama:*   Like many other foods, this has a better flavor if it is not ice cold. Let it stand for 15 to 20 minutes at room temperature before serving.

## Vegetarian Chopped Liver

This has nothing to do with liver, but it is delicious and makes a good appetizer for a meatless meal.

*1 pound green beans, ends*
*   trimmed and strings removed*
*1 medium onion, finely chopped*
*¼ cup corn oil*
*5 hard-boiled eggs, peeled and*
*   roughly chopped*

*1 teaspoon salt*
*Freshly ground black pepper*
*   to taste*

Bring a large kettle of water to the boil. Drop in the green beans and cook until they are just tender but still bright green, about 10 minutes. Drain the beans, cool under cold running water, and drain again.

Sauté onion in corn oil until golden brown. Combine onion with the eggs, cooked green beans, salt and pepper in the bowl of a food processor and process for a few seconds until mixture resembles the texture of chopped chicken liver. Alternatively, chop all the ingredients by hand and mix together well. Cool in refrigerator until ready to serve. Taste for seasoning.

YIELD:   *4 to 6 appetizer servings.*

*Advice from Mama:*   For a nonvegetarian version, without any actual liver in it, try my mother's recipe. She substituted Schmaltz (page 10) and grieben for the corn oil. Cholesterol heaven!

# Eggplant Caviar

I've had this dish made a dozen different ways, but my Russian friend, Raisa, made the best. I took her recipe and improved on it (I think). She may not agree, but since she's kind, she tells me it's delicious.

| | |
|---|---|
| *2 medium eggplants* | *4 garlic cloves* |
| *Kosher salt* | *¼ cup corn oil* |
| *1 large green bell pepper* | *1 small can tomato sauce* |
| *1 large onion* | *1 teaspoon salt or more to taste* |

Trim away tops of eggplants and peel away the skin. Cut the eggplants lengthwise into slices about ½ inch thick. Sprinkle eggplant slices on both sides with kosher salt and arrange the slices in a colander, standing upright against the sides of the colander. Let stand for 30 minutes. Rinse the eggplant slices under cold running water to remove the salt. (This salting process removes any bitterness there may be in the eggplant.)

Preheat oven to 375°F.

Place eggplant slices on foil-lined baking sheet and bake for ½ hour at 375°F. Remove from oven and let cool. When cool enough to handle, chop the eggplant into small pieces.

Remove seeds and core from green pepper and dice. Dice onion and crush garlic. Sauté pepper, onion, and garlic in oil until vegetables are slightly softened. Add chopped eggplant, tomato sauce, and salt. Cook over low heat for about 1 hour, until eggplant is very soft and mixture has thickened. Taste for seasoning and add more salt if needed.

Can be served hot or cold, as a side dish or a wonderful appetizer. Eggplant caviar can be refrigerated for up to 5 or 6 days.

YIELD: *8 to 10 servings.*

# Pickled Beets

Years ago, when I was still in junior high school, I had a friend called Janet. Whenever I went to her house, it was filled with the most tantalizing spicy sweet-and-sour smell. And when her mother came out to say hello, her hands were stained a bright blood red. It turned out that she was making her own pickled beets and selling them to local merchants. She was a recent widow and this was one way that she found she could support her family. Since I adored pickled beets, and Janet's mother's were the best, I always think of them along with love and warm family relations.

*1 bunch fresh beets or large can        ½ cup white or cider vinegar*
*   cooked, sliced beets                 ¼ cup sugar*
*2 teaspoons salt                        1 medium onion, thinly sliced*
*1 cup water*

If you are using fresh beets, cut off tops and stems and scrub under cold running water. Place in pot with water to cover, add 1 teaspoon salt and boil until tender, about 20 minutes. Drain and cool. When beets are cool enough to handle, peel them and slice into rounds about ¼ inch thick.

If you are using canned beets, drain them but reserve the beet juice and use instead of water in the recipe.

Place water (or reserved beet juice from canned beets), vinegar, sugar, and remaining 1 teaspoon salt in saucepan and bring to a boil and cook, stirring, until sugar is dissolved. Mix beets together with sliced onion in a bowl and pour hot marinade over the beets and onions. Cover and refrigerate for 2 days before using. Drain and serve. These beets are also good hot. Heat them first in their liquid, then drain. Serve as a side dish with any meat meal. Pickled beets served with endive make a lovely salad. I was served a similar salad once, years ago, in a wonderful French restaurant in New York.

Y I E L D :   *6 to 8 servings.*

*Advice from Mama:*   I tell you to cook the beets whole and unpeeled for two good reasons. One, you don't lose a lot of the flavor, and the second and best reason is that they're a lot easier to peel when cooked whole.

# Marinated Mushrooms

Making your own marinated mushrooms is very easy and everybody will be impressed with your culinary skills. It's nice to serve them as part of a larger hors d'oeuvres selection with toothpicks on the side so people can spear themselves a mushroom.

| | |
|---|---|
| *1 pound small button mushrooms* | *1 pound large white mushrooms, quartered* |
| *or* | *½ cup corn oil* |

1 cup red wine vinegar
2 cloves garlic, crushed
¼ teaspoon freshly ground
   black pepper

1 small pimento (the kind that
   comes in a jar), chopped fine
1 small onion, chopped very fine
¼ teaspoon dried oregano

Bring about a quart of lightly salted water to a boil. Add the mushrooms and reduce heat to a simmer. Simmer for 3 minutes and drain. In a bowl mix together the oil, vinegar, garlic, pepper, pimento, onion, and oregano. Add the mushrooms and toss well. Marinate for several hours or overnight. Serve at room temperature as part of an appetizer selection.

YIELD:  *6 to 8 servings.*

# Abbas

I'm not sure where the name for these wonderful chick-peas comes from, but that is what my mother called them. When I grew up, I discovered that they are also called "nahit" and that they are a traditional Jewish dish eaten at Purim, or the Feast of Esther.

Whenever my mother made these, my sisters and I would grab the bowl and start munching the chick-peas as if they were peanuts or popcorn. Only these were better. We usually gathered around the radio and listened to "Let's Pretend," or it could have been "The Shadow," while we ate chick-peas until we were in pain. Ahh, but such delicious pain!

6 cups water
1 cup dried chick-peas

Salt
Freshly ground black pepper

Soak chick-peas in water in refrigerator overnight. Drain and rinse. Place in saucepan with enough water to cover by at least 2 inches, bring to a boil and cook at a simmer for 1 to 2 hours, or until chick-peas are very tender. Taste one; if the inside is milky and tender, it's just right. If there is still a "bite" or grainy texture, cook longer.

Drain and place in a bowl. Sprinkle with salt and freshly ground black pepper and toss. Serve warm, like popcorn.

YIELD: *A lot!*

*Advice from Mama:* Unfortunately you cannot substitute canned chick-peas for the dried ones in this recipe. The resulting flavor and texture are just not the same. So make this from scratch, and take my word for it, it'll be worth the trouble.

# Petcha

Although it sounds like the word for a big sneeze, petcha among Jews in Eastern Europe is cholodyetz to Russians, aspic to the English, and gelée to the French. It is meat floating in a cold jellied broth and those who love it do so with a passion.

Whenever my mother made petcha, whoever was home at the time got to suck on the bones, extracting every last drop of delicious broth, marrow, and even tiny bits of meat. If more than one of us was home, there would be a big fight until my mother threatened to banish us from her kitchen. Our kitchen was very much the center of the home. We listened to the radio, did our homework, and played games at the kitchen table while Mama cooked dinner for that night or the next day. Without even knowing that it was happening, I learned about cooking and my mother's ways of preparing our food.

## Clear Petcha

*2 calf's feet, split in half lengthwise and cut across into 1½- to 2-inch chunks (ask your butcher to do this)*

*8 cups water, or enough to cover 2 inches above the bones*
*4 cloves garlic, peeled and sliced*

*1 medium onion, peeled but left whole*
*1 tablespoon kosher salt*
*¼ teaspoon white pepper*

*2 cloves garlic, peeled and crushed*
*1 lemon, cut into wedges*

Wash calf's feet and combine with water, 4 sliced garlic cloves, onion, salt, and pepper in a large kettle. Simmer for 3 to 4 hours, or until meat falls off the bones. At this point approximately 3 to 4 cups water should be left. If not, add more. Add the crushed garlic and simmer for 15 minutes. Remove from heat and let cool. When cool enough to handle, strain broth and discard the solid ingredients. (If you have any hungry children around, let them suck the bones.) Taste the broth and adjust for seasoning. Since it is served cold, it may require a bit more salt. Pour the broth into an 8-by-10-inch glass or ceramic pan (9 by 12 inches is good, too). Refrigerate until firmly jelled. Scrape away any fat that congeals on the top. Cut into squares and serve with lemon wedges, if desired.

## Chunky Petcha

*All the above ingredients plus*
*2 hard-boiled eggs*

Cook as described above. When cool enough to handle, strain the broth, remove meat and cartilege from bones, and extract any marrow from the bones. Cut the meat and cartilage into small pieces. Discard the onion and the bones. Return meat chunks, cartilage, and marrow to broth and pour into an 8-by-10-inch glass or ceramic pan. Peel and slice the hard-boiled eggs and distribute them evenly throughout the mixture. Refrigerate until jelled (overnight is best) and scrape away any fat that congeals on top. Cut into squares and serve with lemon wedges, if desired.

**Ground Meat Petcha**

*Ingredients for Clear Petcha*
*2 hard-boiled eggs*

Cook as for Clear Petcha. When cool enough to handle, strain the broth, remove meat and cartilage from bones and extract any marrow from the bones. Grind the meat, cartilage, and marrow together. Return to liquid and pour into an 8-by-10-inch glass or ceramic pan. Peel and slice the hard-boiled eggs and distribute them evenly throughout the mixture. Refrigerate until firmly jelled (overnight is best). Scrape away any fat that congeals on top. Cut into squares and serve with lemon wedges, if desired.

YIELD:  *8 to 10 slices.*

*Advice from Mama:*  "But, Mama," I can hear you say, "how do I eat this strange dish?" From a plate with a fork, *bubeleh.* By my tastes all you need to go with it is a squeeze or two from a lemon. I know some people have a little horseradish on the side. But I have never approved of this. Why? Because my mother never served it that way.

# Roast Stuffed Derma (Kishke)

What better contribution to *fressen* [eating] have we given the world than the incomparable *kishke* (sections of fire hose)? They tell me my *zadeh* [grandfather] stuffed his own kishke with cow's kishke to the age of 94. He carried around a permanent heartburn which kept his body warm and protected him from the severe Russian winters.

—*Sam Levenson*

Stuffed derma, otherwise known as kishke, is nothing more or less than a particularly delicious Jewish sausage. "Kishke," by the way, means "intestines" in Russian and Yiddish, as in "Oi! Have I got a pain in the kishkes!" Probably from eating too much stuffed derma.

There's no getting around the fact that making stuffed derma requires a lot more work than most of the recipes in this book, but if you love it, it's worth it. Sure, you can buy it ready-made in some Jewish delicatessens, but it will never be as good as this.

Serve stuffed derma hot as a side dish to a meat meal—like brisket or roast chicken, or as an appetizer by itself.

*1 large beef casing or 2 medium*     *1 1/2 cups bread crumbs*
   *beef casings (you will have to*     *1 teaspoon paprika*
   *ask your butcher to order*     *1 tablespoon kosher salt or to*
   *these for you from a kosher*       *taste*
   *supplier)*     *1 teaspoon garlic powder*
*1 large onion, minced*     *1/8 teaspoon white pepper or to*
*1 cup Schmaltz (rendered*       *taste*
   *chicken fat) (page 10)*     *2 large or 3 medium onions,*
*1 1/2 cups matzo meal*       *thinly sliced*

*Prepare the casings:* Soak the casings in heavily salted water (1/2 cup salt to 2 quarts water) for 10 minutes. Rinse casings under cold running water, letting the water run through the inside of the casings.

Sauté the onion in chicken fat until it starts to brown. Mix with matzo meal, bread crumbs, paprika, salt, garlic powder, and pepper. Sew or tie one end of each casing. Fill with stuffing, a little at a time, shaking and squeezing gently so you don't tear the casing. Do not pack too tightly. Sew or tie other end closed.

Preheat oven to 375°F.

Place onions and stuffed derma in a large roasting pan and pour in 3 cups water. Bake in oven for 1 hour. Turn the derma and bake 1 hour longer, until kishkes are nicely browned. Slice and serve.

YIELD: *8 to 12 servings.*

### *Advice from Mama:*

*1.* You can keep any extra beef casings in the freezer indefinitely.
*2.* Should you have any stuffing left over, it will keep in the freezer for a long time.

# Bagel Chips

These make a great and very tasty substitute for crackers. Serve them on their own or with any cheese or dip.

½ cup Clarified Butter (page
   10) or corn oil
4 cloves garlic, crushed

1 teaspoon kosher salt
6 bagels

Preheat oven to 350°F.

Combine clarified butter or corn oil together with garlic and salt. Slice bagels into thinnest possible rounds. You can do this by hand using a very sharp bread knife, but an electric slicer will yield more slices. Brush each round with the flavored butter or oil and arrange the bagel rounds on a baking sheet. Bake for 10 to 12 minutes, until lightly browned. Remove from oven and let cool before serving.

YIELD:  *About 20 to 30 bagel chips.*

*Advice from Mama:*

1. Leave out the garlic, brush with clarified butter or oil, and sprinkle with sesame seeds.
2. Leave out the garlic and substitute 1 small finely minced onion.

# Rye Garlic Toasts

½ cup Clarified Butter (page
   10) or corn oil
4 cloves garlic, crushed
1 teaspoon kosher salt

1 small loaf rye bread (with or
   without caraway seeds your
   choice), sliced

Preheat oven to 350°F.

Combine clarified butter or corn oil together with garlic and salt. Cut each slice of rye bread in half or quarters. Brush each piece with the flavored butter or oil and arrange the rye pieces on a baking sheet. Bake for 10 to 12 minutes, until lightly browned. Remove from oven and let cool before serving.

Y I E L D :  *About 50 to 60 rye toasts.*

# 2

# SOUPS

□ □ □ □ □ □ □ □ □ □ □ □ □ □ □ □

**W**<sup></sup>*hen it comes to* soup, I'm sure that, here, poverty was the mother of invention. When you have a handful of lentils, an onion, and maybe a potato what can you make to feed the family? Only one thing. Soup! Remember the story about the crafty beggar who knocked on a stingy woman's door and begged for a night's lodging? As an inducement he told her he had a magic pot in which he could make a delicious soup from a stone. The woman, who was a big cheapskate, fell for his shtick and invited him in. With a lot of fancy hocus-pocus he set about making soup. He set his pot on the stove, poured in water, and dropped in a stone. After a while he stirred and tasted, rolled his eyes up into his head to show how good the soup was getting, and asked for just a little bit of salt and maybe one onion. In another while the soup was even more delicious but a marrow bone or a piece of chicken wouldn't hurt. They went in. A little while later he asked for some peas and maybe a carrot and a potato. You get the idea. In the end they had a delicious soup and all made from a stone! Before he left the next morning he sold the greedy woman his pot for a pretty penny.

My father used to tell me this story when I was about eleven years old and home sick with pneumonia. My father was home, too, out of work (an all-too-usual occurrence) and taking care of me. It must have been a hard time for my parents, but what did I know then? I loved every minute of it. He would tell me the story and then say, "Do you want me to make you some soup?"

"But, Papa," I said, repeating our standard joke, "I thought all you could make good was pickled herring!"

"Wait and see," he would say, smiling, "wait and see." An hour or more later he returned with a bowl of soup, which he called potato and barley soup and which was always delicious. And it always did have potatoes and barley in it, but the other ingredients varied with his mood and what happened to be on hand. I thought he was the perfect dad and told him so. And he would smile, a huge smile filled with pride and accomplishment. Oh, how I loved my dad!

And, oh, how I still love soup! To me, soup is the perfect food— and certainly the food with the most variety. Just think, soup can be everything from a clear, sparkling broth to a thick pottage in which a wooden spoon can stand. And though I love all kinds of soup, my favorites have always been the ones that with some bread and butter make a meal.

There are not too many rules for cooking soup, but here are a few you should know about:

1. It's just as much trouble to make a little as a lot, so all the recipes are for at least six servings and many make much more than that.
2. Most soups keep well for several days in the refrigerator and are even better reheated.
3. Many soups freeze well, so you can have them on hand whenever you want some. Pour the soup into any size container you prefer, let cool, cover tightly, and freeze.
4. The key words to cooking most soups and stews are "simmer gently." A violent boil will make your soups cloudy. Some

ingredients, like lentils, barley, potatoes, etc., will get mushy if they are boiled for any length of time. Other ingredients, like lima beans, tend to get tough when boiled. So cook your soups over low heat at a gentle simmer—that means the surface of the liquid should get a small bubble only very occasionally. The French call this "making the pot smile"!

You know the expression "in the soup"? Well, it will never apply to you when you add a matzo ball, a knaidlach, or a few kreplach to your lovely clear soup. Rather the opposite will apply, and you will find yourself in everybody's good graces. It is also worth remembering that no good *balabusta* (housewife, or houseperson, in today's world) would ever dare serve a clear soup with nothing in it to cheer it up. Only maybe to a sick person (a very sick person) who was so weak he didn't even have the strength to chew a matzo ball. Otherwise, any good clear soup is simply begging for a few kreplach, a matzo ball or two, a knaidlach, or at least a few mandlen. But what if you're too busy to make some and even your freezer has run out and you're too far away from Mama Leah's take-out? Then at least boil up a few noodles and put them in your soup. Just remember, if you want your soup to stay clear and not muddy-looking, cook the noodles, kreplach, matzo balls, etc., separately in lots of boiling water and slip them into your hot soup at the last minute.

You will find recipes for all kinds of soups in this section and you should try them all, but, always remember, no dish that you will ever cook is as personal as soup. Soup should be what you want it to be, so check out the recipes but then make whatever changes appeal to your own taste. Remember, a clever person can always make soup from a stone.

# Cantaloupe Soup

❖

Let me tell you, this soup is not at all like what my mother or your *bubbie* ever made. It is so rich in flavor and texture you may decide to serve it for dessert! But I have found it to be a very loved soup, especially on a very hot day. It is so rich that the servings should be fairly small, about ½ cup per person.

| | |
|---|---|
| *2 cantaloupes* | *3 cups heavy cream* |
| *2 tablespoons confectioners'* | |
| *sugar* | |

Cut the melons in half. Remove seeds and cut away the rind. Cut one of the melon halves in half again and reserve this quarter of the whole melon for later. Cut the melons into large chunks and place in blender, add sugar and cream, and blend until frothy (about 2 to 3 minutes). You may have to do this in two batches. Cut the reserved one quarter of a melon into tiny pieces and stir into soup. Serve very cold.

Y I E L D : *About 5 cups of soup, making 8 to 10 servings. It is impossible to say exactly how much soup you will get because so much depends on the size and juiciness of the melons.*

<u>*Advice from Mama:*</u> Taste your melons when you cut them open. If they are very sweet, you may wish to cut down on the amount of sugar, or even eliminate it completely.

# Watermelon Soup

❖

This is another delicious and refreshing soup that is good either to start a meal with or to end it. This, too, is a very rich soup and should be served in small quantities, about ½ cup per person.

*¼ of a whole watermelon, rind
  cut away and seeds removed*
*½ of a whole cantaloupe, rind
  cut away and seeds removed*

*2 teaspoons confectioners' sugar*
*2 cups heavy cream*

Cut both melons up in large chunks and reserve a few pieces of watermelon for garnish. Place watermelon and cantaloupe chunks in blender with sugar and cream. You will probably need to do it in two or three batches. Blend until frothy. Cut reserved watermelon into thin slices or small cubes. Serve soup very cold garnished with a few slices or cubes.

Y I E L D : *About 5 cups of soup, making 8 to 10 servings. It is impossible to say exactly how much soup you will get because so much depends on the size and juiciness of the melons.*

*Advice from Mama:*   If the melons are very sweet, reduce or eliminate the sugar.

# Cherry Fruit Soup

My mother always served this as a cold soup before a dairy meal on a hot summer day. The reason is obvious: fresh fruit was inexpensive and readily available in the summertime. She would buy overripe or bruised fruit from the greengrocer and then would wash and cut away the badly bruised areas. She certainly didn't bother removing the pits from the fruit. It was up to each of us to do our own pitting with every mouthful. But I think this is such an elegant and unusual soup that I always take the trouble to remove the pits. Most canned cherries come already pitted.

*4 cups water*
*½ cup sugar*
*¼ teaspoon cinnamon*

*Pinch of cloves*
*1 tablespoon cornstarch*
*1 pound fresh cherries, pitted
  or*

| | |
|---|---|
| *1 16-ounce can tart red cherries in water* | *4 purple plums, stoned and quartered* |
| *4 ripe peaches, stoned and quartered* | *Sour cream or plain yogurt* |

If you are using canned cherries, drain them and replace 1 cup of the water with 1 cup of cherry juice. Place the water, or water and cherry juice, in a saucepan together with sugar, cinnamon, and cloves. Dissolve the cornstarch in a small bowl with ¼ cup of the liquid and add to the water in the saucepan. Bring to a boil and add the cherries, peaches, and plums. Reduce heat to a simmer and cook for 30 minutes.

This soup can be served warm or cold, ungarnished or with a dollop of sour cream or yogurt.

YIELD: *8 servings.*

# Cold Beet Borscht

I never knew of cold beet borscht being served in any way except with a hot potato floating in it. But when I went into the restaurant business I found that it was a problem keeping hot potatoes sitting around waiting for orders of cold beet borscht. So I decided to leave them out. That also turned out to be impossible because anybody that came in looking for cold beet borscht would ask to have it with a hot potato in it. So I got a microwave!

If you serve this to your *zaideh* (grandfather), father, or uncle on a hot summer day (make sure to have a hot potato), he'll kiss and hug you and maybe slip you a little something, you should go buy yourself a nice present.

2 quarts water
8 large beets or 12 small
  (canned beets okay)
1/2 cup sugar
1 medium onion, peeled and cut
  in half

1 tablespoon salt or to taste
Juice of 4 lemons
6 small potatoes
Sour cream

Bring water to a boil. Wash beets thoroughly, scrubbing away any sandy parts. Cut away the root and stem ends and cut beets in half. Add to water. Add sugar, onion, salt, and lemon juice. Simmer for 1 hour or until beets are very tender. Strain beet broth and reserve. Discard the onion pieces. Let beets cool until you can handle them, then peel away the outer skin and discard. You can do this with your fingers. Grate the beets, or process in food processor, and return to reserved beet broth. Let cool and taste for seasoning. Refrigerate until ready to serve.

Half an hour before serving beet borscht, peel and boil the potatoes in lightly salted water until tender. Drain and place one potato in each soup bowl. Ladle cold borscht over hot potatoes and serve immediately with sour cream on the side. This mix of hot and cold is unique to this dish. Once you've tried it, you'll never want to have borscht any other way.

YIELD:  *8 to 10 servings.*

# Schav (Sorrel or Sour Grass Soup)

In most of Eastern Europe sorrel leaves grow wild, and in the spring housewives and children forage in the fields to bring home enough of these tangy green leaves to make this beloved soup. The other name for "sorrel," sour grass, is no joke. Make no mistake, the taste is tart and it wakes up the mouth and gets the juices flowing. To some, this may be an acquired taste, and one I never much cared for myself. But for others, this soup is beloved beyond all others. I always remember my father eating a bowl of schav with such gusto that there could be little doubt as to his opinion of this Old World soup.

| | |
|---|---|
| *1 pound schav (sorrel leaves)* | *2 tablespoons sugar* |
| *2 tablespoons butter or corn oil* | *Juice of 1 lemon* |
| *1 medium onion, finely minced* | *2 egg yolks, beaten* |
| *6 cups water* | *Sour cream* |
| *1 teaspoon kosher salt* | |

Wash the sorrel thoroughly in several changes of cold water. Remove and discard the stems. Chop the leaves into thin ribbons.

Heat the butter or oil in a 3-quart saucepan and sauté the sorrel and onions. Cook, stirring, for 10 minutes. Add water and salt. Let the soup simmer for 25 to 30 minutes. Remove from heat and stir in sugar. Add the lemon juice 1 tablespoon at a time, tasting constantly to achieve the degree of tartness that pleases you. Beat a tablespoon or two of the soup into the egg yolks, then stir egg yolks into the soup. Reheat the soup but do not let it boil after adding the egg yolks.

Serve hot accompanied by sour cream (a dollop or two gets added to each bowl) or cool the soup and chill in refrigerator for several hours or overnight. Serve cold with sour cream.

YIELD: *6 to 8 servings.*

*Advice from Mama:*

1. If you cannot find sorrel, substitute 1 pound fresh spinach and proceed with the recipe exactly as above. You will probably want to add more lemon juice.
2. Add 2 to 3 medium potatoes, peeled and diced, when you are sautéing the sorrel and onions.
3. For a smoother texture, puree all the ingredients before adding lemon juice and egg yolks.

# Carrot Soup (Milchig)

This soup is delicious with heavy cream, but if you are watching calories and fat, substitute evaporated milk for the heavy cream and it will still be very delicious.

*4 tablespoons butter or*
  *margarine*
*2 leeks, cleaned and thinly sliced*
*8 carrots, peeled and cut into*
  *1-inch chunks*
*2 potatoes, peeled and diced*
*4 cups water, approximately*

*1 tablespoon kosher salt*
*Pinch of white pepper*
*1 pint heavy cream or*
  *evaporated milk*
*1 to 2 tablespoons chopped fresh*
  *dill*

Heat the butter or margarine in a 3-quart saucepan and sauté the leeks until they start to turn translucent. Add the carrots, potatoes, enough water to cover everything by 1 inch, and salt and pepper. Simmer, uncovered, for 30 to 40 minutes, until carrots are tender.

Place in blender or food processor and blend to a puree. Pour the pureed soup into a saucepan or tureen and stir in heavy cream or evaporated milk. If serving hot, heat gently but do not allow to boil. If serving cold, chill in the refrigerator for several hours. Serve garnished with a sprinkling of chopped fresh dill.

YIELD: *6 to 8 servings.*

# Bubala's Lox and Potato Soup

When I was eleven years old and recovering from a bout with pneumonia, my aunt Dora, whom I absolutely adored, had me sent up to the Catskills to stay with a cousin who was called Bubala. I don't remember much about my stay except for Bubala's delicious lox and potato soup, which may have had as much to do with my recovery as breathing the mountain air.

Strangely enough, this is the only Jewish fish soup that I have ever come across.

1 large onion, finely diced
4 tablespoons unsalted butter or
    margarine
1 quart milk
4 large potatoes, peeled and
    diced into small pieces

1/4 pound lox or Nova Scotia
    salmon, cut into small pieces
2 wings of the lox, if available*
1/2 teaspoon white pepper

In a 3-quart saucepan, sauté the onion in butter or margarine until it is soft but not brown. Add milk, potatoes, lox, wings of lox, (if using) and pepper. Simmer until potatoes are very soft, about 30 minutes. Make sure the soup does not boil. Remove from heat and taste for seasoning. Remove wings of lox, pick away any cooked lox and place in soup, and discard the wings. Taste for seasoning. If the lox was not salty, the soup may need some salt.

YIELD:   6 servings.

_Advice from Mama:_   I'm against violence in cooking in general, but most soups and stews in particular should never be cooked at a violent boil. A gentle simmer is what's needed for the soup ingredients to develop a full flavor without losing their texture and integrity. Milk should never be boiled because it will foam up and boil over and make a mess and a smell you won't believe. Fish, too, should always be cooked on a gentle heat. So keep your heat low enough for the liquid to cook at the gentlest simmer.

* If you are buying your lox from a deli where they slice it fresh, ask to buy the wings, which are usually discarded. They are the large fins that are cut away to allow for easier slicing.

# Cream of Broccoli Soup

*2 bunches of broccoli*
*2 medium onions, diced*
*4 cloves garlic, crushed*
*¼ cup corn oil or butter*
*2 quarts chicken stock or water*

*2 large Knorr chicken bouillon*
  *cubes (omit if using stock)*
*1 pint heavy cream*
*1 tablespoon kosher salt, if*
  *needed*

Wash the broccoli and trim away leaves and the very woody stem ends. Peel the stems up to where the bud branches begin. Separate broccoli head into flowerets and slice the stalks and stems into ¼-inch pieces. In a large (4½- to 5-quart) soup kettle, sauté the onions and garlic in corn oil or butter until soft but not browned. Add chicken stock, or water and bouillon cubes, and the broccoli, reserving 2 large flowerets. Simmer the soup for 30 minutes, until broccoli is tender. Add the reserved flowerets and cook for 5 minutes longer. Place in blender with cream (you will probably have to do this in two batches) and puree. Taste for seasoning and add salt if necessary. Serve hot or cold.

YIELD:  *8 to 10 servings.*

*Advice from Mama:*  The reason for adding the reserved broccoli flowerets for only the last 5 minutes of cooking is that they give the soup a vivid green coloring and bits of crispy texture that are most pleasing to the eye and palate.

# Cream of Mushroom Soup

There was a time when many housewives discovered that there was a certain brand of canned cream of mushroom soup that could be used to make an all-purpose sauce for any number of stews, casseroles, and even vegetable dishes. As a result everything from string beans to tuna casserole began to taste the same, and good, old-fashioned, blameless cream of mushroom soup acquired a reputation for being just a little "tacky." But never mind. Forget the cans and try this easy, made-from-scratch mushroom soup and you will understand why it got so popular to begin with.

*6 tablespoons butter or corn oil* *4 tablespoons all-purpose flour*
*1 small onion, finely diced*  *4 cups half-and-half*
*½ pound mushrooms, thinly*  *1 teaspoon salt*
 *sliced*        *¼ teaspoon white pepper*

Heat 2 tablespoons butter or oil in a skillet and sauté the onion until it turns a rich golden brown, 20 to 30 minutes. Add the sliced mushrooms and sauté 2 to 3 minutes more, until the mushrooms soften and give up some of their juice.

Heat remaining 4 tablespoons butter or oil in a 3-quart saucepan. Stir in the 4 tablespoons flour and cook, stirring constantly, to make a golden roux. This will take about 3 minutes. Do not let the roux turn brown. Gradually add the half-and-half, and use a whisk to beat the liquid into the roux. Do this over low, steady heat and continue beating with a whisk until all the liquid has been incorporated into the roux. Simmer for about 10 minutes, stirring frequently, until mixture thickens. Stir in the onions and mushrooms, salt and pepper. Allow to heat through, but do not boil.

YIELD: *4 to 6 servings.*

*Advice from Mama:* You can replace some or all of the half-and-half with evaporated milk or even regular milk.

# Cabbage Soup

2 onions, coarsely chopped
1 carrot, peeled and thinly sliced
2 tablespoons corn oil
6 cups beef broth (can be made
  from bouillon cubes)
1 small head of cabbage,
  shredded
½ cup sauerkraut, rinsed under
  cold running water and
  coarsely chopped

1 ripe tomato, peeled and cut
  into chunks
or
1 cup canned Italian-style
  tomatoes, cut into chunks
1 clove garlic, crushed
2 cups water
Salt, if necessary
Lemon wedges (optional)

Sauté onions and carrot in corn oil in the bottom of a 5-quart soup kettle, until softened, about 10 minutes. Combine with remaining ingredients (except for lemon wedges) and simmer over low heat, covered, but with lid slightly askew for 50 minutes. Taste for salt and serve in hot bowls. Serve with lemon wedges if desired.

YIELD: *6 to 8 servings.*

*Advice from Mama:*

1. This soup is very good reheated on the day after cooking and even the day after that. The flavors seem to get better and better. Also, you can put this soup up in a plastic container and freeze to have on hand for a quick lunch or dinner.
2. You can add a couple of peeled, diced potatoes to this soup if you wish, but don't freeze soup with potatoes in it. Potatoes are the only vegetable I know that do not freeze well—they get very mushy.
3. If you're feeding vegetarians, substitute broth made from vegetable bouillon cubes for the beef broth.

# Mushroom-Barley Soup

### ❧

Barley soup always reminds me of the fairy tale where the cup just kept running over. When you cook barley it seems never to stop expanding. Even when you've stopped cooking, if the soup is refrigerated overnight, you will need more liquid when you reheat it. But mushroom-barley soup is one of the most comforting, *haimish* soups I know. I like to serve it as a meal by itself, in large bowls with rye toast and lots of butter.

*¼ cup corn or vegetable oil*
*1 large onion, diced*
*2 stalks celery, diced small*
*4 cloves garlic, crushed*
*3 quarts beef broth or chicken broth*

*1 cup pearl barley, rinsed under cold running water*
*2 carrots, peeled and diced*
*2 pounds mushrooms, sliced*
*¼ teaspoon pepper*
*Salt to taste*

Heat the oil in the bottom of a 5- or 6-quart soup kettle and sauté the onion, celery, and garlic until vegetables start to turn transparent, but not browned (about 10 minutes). Add broth, barley, carrots, and mushrooms. Simmer gently, stirring from time to time, until barley is tender, about 2 hours. If soup gets too thick, add more broth or water. Taste for seasoning, add pepper and salt if necessary. Serve hot.

YIELD: *10 to 12 servings.*

*Advice from Mama:*

1. You can, if you like, substitute ½ cup dried mushrooms for 1 pound of fresh mushrooms. Soak the dried mushrooms in hot water to cover for 20 minutes, strain and add to soup. You can strain the mushroom soaking water through a paper coffee filter and substitute it for an equal amount of the broth. Dried mushrooms have a more intense, woodsy flavor and will give a rich taste to this soup.
2. This recipe makes a lot of soup, but the soup is good for several days and freezes well also.

# Potato-Mushroom Soup

This is a very delicious Old World soup. The combination of lima beans, mushrooms, and potatoes is very earthy and satisfying. This soup can definitely make a meal, and if you substitute vegetable broth made from vegetable bouillon cubes, it is a great meal if you're trying to please some vegetarians.

½ cup dried baby lima beans
6 cups cold water
¼ cup corn or vegetable oil
1 large onion, diced
2 stalks celery, diced small
4 cloves garlic, crushed
3 quarts beef broth or chicken broth

2 carrots, peeled and diced
2 pounds mushrooms, sliced
4 large Idaho potatoes, peeled and diced
¼ teaspoon pepper
Salt to taste

Soak the baby lima beans in water overnight. Drain and rinse the beans before adding them to the soup.

Heat the oil in the bottom of 5-quart soup kettle and sauté the onion, celery, and garlic until vegetables start to turn transparent, but not browned (about 10 minutes). Add broth, lima beans, carrots, and mushrooms. Simmer gently, stirring from time to time, until lima beans are tender, about 1½ to 2 hours. Add the potatoes after the soup has cooked for 1 hour. If soup gets too thick, add more broth or water. Taste for seasoning, add pepper and salt if necessary. Serve hot.

YIELD: *10 to 12 servings.*

*Advice from Mama:*

1. You can, if you like, substitute ½ cup dried mushrooms for 1 pound of fresh mushrooms. Soak the dried mushrooms in hot water to cover for 20 minutes, strain and add to soup. You can strain the mushroom soaking water through a paper coffee filter and substitute it for an equal amount of the broth. Dried

mushrooms have a more intense, woodsy flavor and will give a rich taste to this soup.

2. This soup keeps well for several days in the refrigerator and becomes more delicious every time you reheat it. It does not, however, freeze very well, because of the potatoes.

## Potato-Barley Soup

I always think of my father when I make potato-barley soup, because this is the soup he made for me whenever I was home sick. And it's the kind of comforting, easy-to-digest soup that anyone would like to have when they're sick, or maybe just a little tired.

*1/4 cup corn or vegetable oil*
*1 large onion, diced*
*2 stalks celery, diced small*
*4 cloves garlic, crushed*
*3 quarts beef broth or chicken broth*
*1/2 cup pearl barley, rinsed under cold running water*

*2 carrots, peeled and diced*
*2 large Idaho potatoes, peeled and diced small*
*1/4 teaspoon pepper*
*Salt to taste*

Heat the oil in the bottom of a 5-quart soup kettle and sauté the onion, celery, and garlic until vegetables start to turn transparent, but not browned (about 10 minutes). Add broth, barley, and carrots. Simmer gently, stirring from time to time, until barley is tender, about 2 hours. Add the potatoes after the soup has cooked for 1 hour. If soup gets too thick, add more broth or water. Taste for seasoning, add pepper and salt if necessary. Serve hot.

YIELD: *10 to 12 servings.*

*Advice from Mama:* You can make this a purely vegetarian soup by substituting vegetable broth made from vegetable bouillon cubes for the beef or chicken broth.

# Lentil Soup

There's no doubt about it, lentils go back a long, long way—all the way to the Bible, in fact. Esau sold his birthright for a dish of lentils and I only hope that soup was as good as the one I make all the time. Sometimes I leave out the chicken broth and bouillon cubes for a nice vegetarian version. That, too, is very delicious and with good, dark bread can make a whole meal.

*2 cups lentils*
*¼ cup corn oil*
*2 medium onions, diced fine*
*2 stalks celery*
*2 cloves garlic, crushed*
*2 quarts water or chicken broth*

*2 large Knorr chicken bouillon cubes (eliminate bouillon cubes if using broth)*
*4 carrots, peeled and diced*
*Salt to taste*

Pick over lentils to remove any stones or debris. Put them in a large pot and wash them in several changes of cold water. Drain and set aside. (You can eliminate this step if the package says lentils are washed and presorted.)

Heat the corn oil in the bottom of a 4-quart soup kettle. Sauté onions, celery, and garlic until vegetables become translucent. Add water or chicken stock, bouillon cubes, carrots, and lentils. Simmer for 1½ to 2 hours or until lentils are very tender. If the soup gets too thick, thin it out with a little water or chicken broth until it is the consistency you like. Taste and add salt if you think it needs some.

Y I E L D :   *8 to 10 servings.*

*Advice from Mama:*

1. You may substitute vegetable bouillon cubes for a very nice vegetarian soup.
2. You can freeze this soup to have on hand whenever you want some.

# Split Pea Soup

2 cups split peas
¼ cup corn oil
2 medium onions, diced fine
2 stalks celery
2 cloves garlic, crushed
2 quarts water or chicken broth

2 large Knorr chicken bouillon
 cubes (eliminate bouillon
 cubes if using broth)
4 carrots, peeled and diced
Salt to taste

Pick over peas to remove any stones or debris. Put them in a large pot and wash them in several changes of cold water. Drain and set aside. (You can eliminate this step if the package says peas are washed and presorted.)

Heat the corn oil in the bottom of a 4-quart soup kettle. Sauté onions, celery, and garlic until vegetables become translucent. Add water or chicken stock, bouillon cubes, carrots, and peas. Simmer gently for 1½ to 2 hours or until peas are very tender. If the soup gets too thick, thin it out with a little water or chicken broth until it is the consistency you like. Taste and add salt if you think it needs some.

YIELD: *8 to 10 servings.*

*Advice from Mama:*

1. You may substitute vegetable bouillon cubes for a very nice vegetarian soup.
2. You can freeze this soup to have on hand whenever you want some.

# Romanian Bean Soup
# (Vegetarian)

If you like the flavor of lima beans, which I do, then you'll love this thick, hearty soup.

2 cups dried lima beans
8 cups cold water
1 large onion, roughly chopped
1 carrot, peeled and quartered
2 cloves garlic, crushed
1 Knorr vegetable bouillon cube

2 tablespoons corn oil
1 medium onion, finely diced
2 teaspoons kosher salt
  (optional)
Freshly ground black pepper
  to taste

Soak lima beans in cold water overnight. Drain the lima beans and rinse in several changes of water to float away as many loosened shells as possible. Place in a 5-quart soup kettle with 8 cups fresh water, the chopped onion, carrot, garlic, and bouillon cube. Simmer gently for 1 to 1½ hours, until beans are very tender. Remove from heat and let cool a little.

In the meantime heat the oil in a skillet and sauté the finely diced onion until it is very brown. Ladle a small amount of soup at a time into blender or the bowl of a food processor and puree. Return to pot and stir in browned onions. Taste for seasoning and add salt and pepper to taste.

YIELD:  *8 to 10 servings.*

*Advice from Mama:*

1. When reheating leftover soup that has been refrigerated, you may wish to add a little more water or broth (about ½ cup) because the soup thickens as it stands.
2. You can freeze this soup to have on hand whenever you want some.

# Hearty Lima Bean Soup

This soup is a variation of the recipe for Romanian Bean Soup. Served with good bread and a salad, it makes a hearty meal-in-one.

My mother's version, which she called "bebbela" (bean) soup, was a little different. She never pureed it, but used large lima beans that my father and I had to shell after they were soaked overnight. My mother insisted that this made for a more tender and digestible soup. She was probably right, but who wants to spend time shelling beans?

*2 cups dried lima beans*
*8 cups cold water*
*1 pound lean chuck or bottom*
*   round*
*1 large onion, roughly chopped*
*1 carrot, scraped and quartered*

*2 cloves garlic, crushed*
*2 teaspoons kosher salt*
*2 tablespoons corn oil*
*1 medium onion, finely diced*
*Freshly ground black pepper*
*   to taste*

Soak lima beans in cold water overnight. Drain and rinse in several changes of cold water. Place in a 5-quart soup kettle with 8 cups fresh water, the meat, onion, carrot, garlic, and salt. Simmer gently for 1 to 1½ hours, until beans are very tender. Remove from heat and let cool.

In the meantime heat the oil in a skillet and sauté the finely diced onion until it is very brown. Remove meat from soup to a platter or cutting board and cut into bite-size pieces. Ladle a small amount of soup at a time into blender or the bowl of a food processor and puree. Return to pot, add the meat, and stir in browned onions. Taste for seasoning and add pepper to taste. Reheat if necessary and serve hot.

YIELD: *8 servings.*

*Advice from Mama:*   Instead of the meat, add 1 chicken that has been quartered. Remove the chicken before pureeing the soup. Take the meat from the bone and discard the skin. Pull meat apart with your fingers into bite-size pieces and return to the pureed soup.

# Mama Leah's Chicken Soup

The chicken is to Jewish cooking what pork is to Chinese cuisine. It reigns supreme. Nothing is wasted, every last bit is used. The fat is rendered and turned to schmaltz, the livers are transformed into a tasty appetizer, the wrinkled skin that covers the chicken's neck is stuffed and roasted to make a tasty dish called Helzel (page 131), and the rest of the chicken is cooked in as many different ways as there are Jewish cooks. But certainly the most popular, the most enduring, the most sustaining dish ever made from any chicken is to turn it into a golden, glorious chicken soup. Everybody has heard it called Jewish penicillin, but it is also Jewish Pepto-Bismol, Jewish aspirin, and even Jewish Valium. No less a person than the twelfth-century Jewish philosopher Maimonides had this to say about chicken soup: "As far as possible the meat [eaten] should be that of hens or roosters and their broth should also be taken, because this sort of fowl has virtue in rectifying corrupted humors, whatever the corruption may be, and especially the black humours, so much so that the physicians have mentioned that chicken broth is beneficial in leprosy."

This is it, then, the indispensable miracle of Jewish cooking, Mama's personal panacea, the Band-Aid for whatever ails you: chicken soup.

1 large broiler chicken (3½ to 4
  pounds), cut into 8 pieces
7 to 8 cups water, or just
  enough to cover chicken and
  vegetables
3 stalks celery with their leaves
3 carrots, peeled but left whole
2 parsnips, peeled
1 large or 2 small leeks
  (substitute 1 medium onion if
  leeks are not available)

½ bunch parsley, stems
  included
½ bunch fresh dill, stems
  included
1 tablespoon kosher salt
1 teaspoon white pepper
1 clove garlic, peeled but left
  whole

Wash chicken pieces well and remove any quills or pinfeathers. Pull away any visible excess fat. Do not remove the skin because the skin adds flavor to the soup. Place chicken in a 6-quart soup kettle and add 8 cups cold water. Wash celery and cut each stalk in half crosswise and add to pot. Cut each carrot in half crosswise, then cut down the middle, making 12 pieces. Add the carrots to the pot. Cut the parsnips in half lengthwise and add these to the pot. Trim the ends off the leeks, cut in half lengthwise, and wash carefully under cold running water, separating the layers to remove all the grit. Cut leeks in half crosswise and add to the pot. Wash parsley and dill and add to pot along with the salt, pepper, and garlic clove. Add more water if needed, to just cover the chicken and the vegetables.

Bring to a boil and immediately lower heat to a simmer. Cook for 10 minutes and skim away the scum that forms on the top. Simmer gently, uncovered, for 1 hour longer.

Skim away any fat that has risen to the surface of the soup or degrease the broth in a degreasing pitcher (see Advice from Mama, below). Of course, if you have the time, you can simply chill the soup until the fat congeals and remove it that way.

There are several ways you can serve this chicken soup. My mother would remove the greens and vegetables and the chicken pieces. The soup would be strained to a clear broth and served as its own course with noodles, Matzo Balls (see page 209), or Kreplach (see page 66). The soup greens were transformed into delicious Latkes (see page 113) and served as a side dish along with the boiled chicken. I like to serve everything all together in a large bowl, the broth, the veggies, the chicken, and throw in a couple of kreplach, matzo balls, and noodles. I call it Chicken in the Pot and there's nothing like it for curing colds, tummy aches, or even just a plain bad mood.

YIELD: *4 servings as a main dish or 8 to 10 for just soup.*

*Advice from Mama:*

1. Degreasing broths and other liquids: If you want to remove every last bit of fat floating in the soup, pour the soup through a strainer to separate the liquid from the solid ingredients.

Then pour the liquid through a glass or plastic degreasing pitcher that has a spout coming up from the bottom. These are marvelous gadgets that instantly separate the fat from the liquid and allow you to pour off the liquid, which is then completely fat-free. You can find degreasing pitchers in stores that sell cooking supplies and in cookware catalogs as well. The kind I use is called Souper Strain and is manufactured by East Hampton Industries. You can buy it from them by mail, by calling (800) 645-1188.

2. Even though it violates my rule of one-pot cooking, you should always cook kreplach, matzo balls, and noodles separately in boiling water, then add to the soup. This makes everything taste better and keeps the soup clear. Besides, you've been in the kitchen so long already, what's a few more minutes going to hurt you?

3. If you want more soup, get a bigger chicken. An oven stuffer roaster, for example, that weighs 5 to 6 pounds is good. Have the butcher cut it up, add a few cups more water, keep everything else the same. Or throw in another carrot and whatever other vegetables you want. This is soup, not béarnaise sauce.

## Kreplach (Jewish Wonton)

Soup could offer a variety of surprises—*kreplach* (meat balls with sport jackets), exquisitely shaped by the sculptural genius of a *balabusteh* [housewife], who always planned the structure of the *kreple* so that a tempting bit of the buried treasure should show through, just enough to make the mouth water.

*—Sam Levenson*

I suppose it is true that it takes a little bit of time and trouble to make kreplach, but it's not hard and you can make them ahead of time, at your leisure, and keep them in the freezer ready to cook at a moment's notice. Incidentally, some Jews interpret the tradition of eating kreplach at Yom Kippur symbolically: the dough enfolds the filling just as God's mercy enfolds our fate and fortune for the coming year.

## Noodle Dough

2 cups all-purpose flour, plus
  additional flour for rolling out
  the dough

2 large eggs, beaten
½ teaspoon salt
1½ tablespoons water

Measure the flour into a large bowl. Make a hole in the middle of the flour and pour in the beaten eggs, salt, and water. Mix with a wooden spoon until dough starts to hold together, then remove dough to a well-floured board and knead until it feels smooth and satiny. Cover the dough and let it rest for 30 minutes.

## Meat Filling

1 pound (approximately) chuck
  or brisket, or same amount of
  leftover cooked meat
1 onion, diced fine
½ cup Schmaltz (rendered
  chicken fat) (page 10)

1 teaspoon salt
⅛ teaspoon freshly ground
  black pepper
1 clove garlic, crushed

Preheat oven to 375°F.

Buy a piece of chuck or brisket weighing about 1 pound and cut it into 6 chunks, all about the same size. Put in a small roasting pan or ovenproof dish and roast in oven for 45 minutes. Sauté the onion in the chicken fat until it starts to turn golden brown. Put the roasted meat, together with the sautéed onions, through a meat grinder, or grind in food processor. Add the salt, pepper, and garlic and mix well. Taste for seasoning and adjust.

## Making the Kreplach

Divide the dough into two parts. Cover one part and set aside. Roll out the other dough on a well-floured board until it is about ⅛ inch thick.

Cut the dough into 3-inch squares. Place about 2 teaspoons of filling onto the center of each square. Fold into a triangle and seal by pinching the sides closed with your fingertips. It helps to keep your hands lightly floured. Place kreplach onto a floured tray or cookie sheet and cover to keep from drying out. Repeat with the remaining dough.

## Freezing the Kreplach

Arrange the kreplach in one layer on waxed paper on a metal cookie sheet and place, uncovered, in the freezer. When kreplach have frozen, remove from cookie sheet, place them in a plastic freezer bag or airtight container, and seal tightly. Do not thaw before cooking, simply add about 5 minutes to the cooking time.

## Cooking the Kreplach

Bring a large pot of salted water to a boil, add 1 tablespoon oil and drop the kreplach into it, but no more than will float in one layer, about 8 kreplach at a time. Reduce the heat to a simmer and cook for 10 to 12 minutes. Remove the kreplach with a large slotted spoon and keep them warm. Repeat until all the kreplach you want are cooked.

Serve kreplach in soup or fry them and serve as an appetizer.

## Fried Kreplach

Boil kreplach as described. Drain on paper towels to remove excess water. Sauté in corn oil or chicken fat until they are crispy brown.

YIELD: *30 to 40 kreplach.*

# Chicken in the Pot

You will want to have very large soup bowls for this meal-in-one, although what you really want to have is a good friend and wonderful potter like Elizabeth Nields, who made up a set of beautiful individual soup tureens with covers for me.

*3 small chickens (3 to 3½
    pounds each), split in half*
*Chicken gizzards without the
    livers (optional)*
*6 celery stalks, each broken in
    half*
*6 carrots, peeled and trimmed,
    each cut in half and split*
*3 to 4 parsnips, peeled and split
    in two*
*2 leeks or 2 medium onions,
    diced large*
*1 bunch fresh dill, heavy stems*

*removed*
*1 bunch parsley, heavy stems
    removed*
*1 tablespoon salt*
*1 teaspoon white pepper*
*1 clove garlic, peeled*
*Water to cover*
*12 cooked Matzo Balls (page
    209) (optional)*
*12 cooked Kreplach (page
    66) (optional)*
*8 ounces cooked thin noodles
    (optional)*

Wash the chickens and remove all visible fat. Do not remove the skin because the skin adds flavor to the soup. Wash the gizzards. Place celery, carrots, parsnips, and leeks or onions in an 8-quart soup kettle. Place the halved chickens on top and add the gizzards, dill, parsley, salt, pepper, and garlic. Add enough water to cover chicken with one inch to spare.

Bring to a boil and immediately reduce to a simmer. Skim away any scum that rises to the top. Place cover on the pot slightly askew and simmer gently for about 1 hour or until the chicken is tender.

Skim away any visible fat or degrease the broth (see page 65 for details).

To serve, place 2 cooked matzo balls, and/or 2 cooked kreplach, and/or ½ cup cooked thin noodles in a large bowl. Add a cooked chicken half and soup. Divide the vegetables among the bowls. Serve hot with challah or another good bread. This makes a great meal!

Y I E L D :   *6 servings for good eaters, 10 servings for picky ones.*

# Beef Broth

A cup of hot, clear, homemade beef broth is one of the most restorative soups you could have. It makes a very elegant beginning to any dinner and is also good in the middle of a winter afternoon to just perk you up.

*4 pounds beef shinbones, with*
*meat on bones*
*2 pounds marrow bones*
*5 quarts water*
*2 cloves garlic, peeled and*
*quartered*
*1 large onion, peeled and*
*quartered*

*2 carrots, peeled and halved*
*3 stalks celery, cut in half*
*1 bay leaf*
*1 tablespoon salt*
*6 black peppercorns*
*or*
*¼ teaspoon ground pepper*

Place all the ingredients in a 10-quart soup kettle or stockpot. Bring to a boil and immediately reduce heat to a simmer. Skim off any scum that rises to the top. Simmer the broth for 1 ½ to 2 hours, stirring occasionally with a long-handled wooden spoon to make sure that the bones are not scorching on the bottom of the pot. Remove and discard the bones. If you have any marrow bones, remove the marrow and have a nice snack. Strain the broth and discard all the vegetables. Pour the broth into plastic containers and place in refrigerator, uncovered, until the fat congeals. Remove and discard the fat. Alternatively, degrease the broth according to instructions on page 65.

Serve plain or with kasha in the broth for a nourishing soup on a cold day. Or freeze and use as a delicious soup base in any of the recipes that call for beef broth.

YIELD: *About 4 quarts broth.*

*Advice from Mama:*

1. Beef broth (like chicken broth) freezes extremely well and if you have containers of either one in your freezer, it's like having money in the bank.
2. If you would like to serve clear beef broth for the start of a fancy dinner, you can dress it up with a sprinkling of finely chopped parsley or dill.

# Bean and Barley Soup

*6 cups water*
*1 cup dried lima or navy beans*
*1 large onion, diced*
*2 stalks celery, diced*
*4 cloves garlic, crushed*
*1/4 cup corn or vegetable oil*

*3 quarts beef or chicken broth*
*   or water*
*1/2 cup pearl barley*
*2 carrots, peeled and diced*
*1 tablespoon kosher salt or to*
*   taste*

Soak beans in water overnight. Drain and rinse in several changes of cold water.

Sauté the onion, celery, and garlic in corn or vegetable oil until vegetables start to turn transparent, but not browned (about 10 minutes). Transfer to a 5-quart soup kettle, add broth or water, barley, carrots, and beans. Bring to a boil, then simmer slowly, stirring frequently until beans are tender, about 2 hours. Taste and add salt if necessary.

YIELD:   *8 to 12 servings.*

*Advice from Mama:*   I recently read that you can avoid gastric distress from eating beans by changing the soaking water several times. So if you suffer from gas, try this.

# Cabbage Borscht

My father and I both loved cabbage borscht and thought that my mother made the best there ever was. Today everyone thinks my soup is great, but in my memory my mother's cabbage borscht was much better. This soup always tastes best when made a day ahead. This also gives you a chance to easily remove any fat, and the flavors improve by sitting.

*1 large green cabbage (about 3 pounds) or 2 medium cabbages (1½ pounds each)*
*4 large beets, peeled and diced (canned are okay)*
*2 medium onions, diced*
*8 cloves garlic*

*4 flanken or 8 short ribs*
*⅓ cup brown sugar*
*¾ cup ketchup*
*1 tablespoon kosher salt*
*Juice of 2 lemons*
*3 quarts cold water, or more if needed*

Remove and discard the large outer leaves of the cabbage. Wash it and cut into quarters. Cut away the cores and cut cabbage quarters into ½-inch slices. Place into a 6-quart soup kettle. Peel and dice the beets and onions, and crush the garlic. Add them to the cabbage. Add the flanken or short ribs, sugar, ketchup, salt, and lemon juice. Add water to cover all the ingredients by 2 inches.

Bring to a boil and immediately reduce heat to a simmer. Skim away any scum that rises to the surface. Simmer gently for about 2 hours, or until the flanken is fork tender. Remove the flanken or short ribs from the soup. Cut the meat away from the bones, removing any fat and gristle. Return the meat to the soup and discard the bones. If you are serving it the following day, let it cool completely and refrigerate. Remove any fat that has come to the surface before reheating. If you are serving it immediately, skim away any fat that has risen to the surface before serving.

This makes a great meal-in-one, with salad and bread. Pumpernickel and rye are my favorites.

Y I E L D :   *6 servings as a main course; 8 to 10 servings for soup course.*

### Advice from Mama:

1. If fresh beets are not available, substitute canned beets and add for last 15 minutes of cooking time.
2. A little fresh dill sprinkled in each plate just before serving is always nice.

# Sauerkraut Soup (Kapusniak)

Sauerkraut soup may sound strange to you at first, but when you think of the many past generations of people who survived the winter thanks to stores of sauerkraut, you may think of this humble vegetable with more respect. Cooking sauerkraut for a long time gives it a wonderful mild flavor, and the resulting soup is very delicious indeed.

*1 pound sauerkraut, fresh, canned, or packaged*
*2 pounds flanken or short ribs*
*1/2 cup brown sugar*
*2 cloves garlic, crushed*

*1 pound canned tomatoes*
*4 cups water or enough to cover ingredients by 1 inch*
*6 gingersnaps, crushed (optional)*

Place all the ingredients, except the gingersnaps, in a 5-quart soup kettle and add water to cover. Simmer for 2 to 2½ hours, stirring frequently, until meat is fork tender. Thirty minutes before soup is done, add the crushed gingersnaps. When the soup is done, remove the flanken and/or short ribs. Skim away as much fat as possible from the soup. If you have time, refrigerate soup overnight and remove all the congealed fat. Or follow instructions for degreasing, page 65. Cut the meat away from the bone and into bite-size pieces, cutting away any fat and gristle. Return meat to the soup. Reheat if necessary.

YIELD: *6 to 8 servings.*

# Potato-Beef Soup

| | |
|---|---|
| *2 pounds chuck or bottom round* | *¼ cup barley* |
| *2 marrow bones (optional)* | *4 cloves garlic, crushed* |
| *4 quarts water* | *1 bay leaf* |
| *1 large onion, finely diced* | *1 tablespoon salt* |
| *2 carrots, peeled and finely diced* | *¼ teaspoon freshly ground* |
| *2 stalks celery, finely diced* | *black pepper, or to taste* |
| | *6 large Idaho or russet potatoes* |

Place all the ingredients except the potatoes in an 8-quart soup kettle. Bring to a boil and immediately reduce to a simmer. Skim away any scum that rises to the top. Simmer gently for 2½ to 3 hours, stirring from time to time to make sure nothing is scorching on the bottom of the pot. Peel and dice the potatoes and add them to the soup after 2 hours. When meat and potatoes are tender remove soup from heat. Skim away any visible fat floating on the top of the soup. Remove the marrow bones, pick out the marrow and return to the soup. Discard the bones and bay leaf. Remove the meat, cut into bite-size pieces and return to the soup. Serve hot, in large bowls, as a delicious meal-in-one.

YIELD: *6 to 8 servings.*

*Advice from Mama:* An interesting variation on this soup is to substitute 1 cup of baby lima beans, soaked in water to cover overnight, for the barley.

# Carrot Soup (Flaischig)

Whenever my mother made a soup using marrow bones, my father and I had a field day. Despite the rude noises we made, we loved sucking out the marrow left in the bones. What a delicacy! If you love marrow, indulge yourself and not the soup. After all, you did the cooking.

*¼ cup corn oil*
*2 large onions, diced*
*2 stalks celery, diced*
*4 cloves garlic, crushed*
*1 tablespoon kosher salt*
*10 carrots, peeled and diced*

*2 potatoes, peeled and diced*
*6 marrow bones or any other*
*    bones for soup*
*¼ teaspoon white pepper*
*Fresh dill, for garnish*

Heat the oil in the bottom of a 5- or 6-quart soup kettle and sauté the onion, celery, and garlic until vegetables start to turn translucent. Add remaining ingredients, except for pepper, with enough water to cover everything by 2 inches. Bring to a boil and immediately lower to a simmer. Cover partially and simmer for 1 to 1½ hours, stirring frequently to prevent scorching. When the soup is done, remove from heat. Remove the bones, remove any marrow and return the marrow to the soup. Discard the bones. Place soup in blender and blend to a puree. Skim off any fat that rises to the top. Taste for seasoning, add pepper and salt if necessary. Serve hot, garnished with fresh dill.

YIELD: *6 to 8 servings.*

*Advice from Mama:* This soup freezes and reheats beautifully.

# Carrot–Lima Bean Soup

This was another favorite soup of mine that my mother made. Somehow the combination of beef and chicken makes this an especially tasty soup. If you prefer, you can substitute a mix of chicken broth and beef broth instead of using chicken and bones. This will also be delicious but a little less hearty. My version makes a complete meal, just add some crusty rye or pumpernickel.

*8 cups cold water*
*2 cups dried baby lima beans*
*½ cup pearl barley*
*2 bunches carrots, about 10 to*
*    12, peeled and diced*
*2 stalks celery, roughly chopped*
*2 medium onions, finely*
*    chopped*

*4 cloves garlic, crushed*
*2 marrow bones (optional)*
*3 quarts water*
*1 tablespoon kosher salt*
*½ teaspoon white pepper*
*Small chicken (2½ to 3*
*    pounds), split in half*

Soak dried baby lima beans in cold water overnight.

Wash barley until water runs clear. Drain the lima beans and rinse in several changes of cold water. Place barley and lima beans in a 6-quart soup kettle together with carrots, celery, onions, garlic, marrow bones if desired, water, salt, and pepper. Simmer gently for 1 hour, stirring frequently. Add the chicken and more water if necessary—there should be enough to just cover everything—and cook for 1 hour longer, until lima beans are tender and chicken is cooked. Remove marrow bones and discard. Remove chicken and cut into smaller pieces. Return to soup and serve as a meal-in-one.

YIELD: *10 to 12 servings.*

# Krupnik (Vegetable-Barley Soup)

The original krupnik, eaten almost daily in nineteenth-century Russian and Polish ghettos, was a much simpler soup, with little or no meat and a lot more barley and potatoes. There were an awful lot of things they didn't have in the way of food and worldly goods, but there was always barley and potatoes. My version is, of course, more modern, but it, too, will make a very hearty, satisfying meal-in-one. When you eat krupnik for dinner, you don't need much else.

*1 pound lean chuck, cut into small cubes*
*1 large onion, diced*
*¼ cup pearl barley*
*¼ cup navy beans, soaked in cold water overnight*
*5 carrots, peeled and diced small*

*1 16-ounce can stewed tomatoes*
*4 cloves garlic, crushed*
*½ pound mushrooms, sliced*
*2 large potatoes, peeled and diced small*
*½ teaspoon freshly ground black pepper*
*Salt to taste*

Place the meat, onion, barley, beans, carrots, tomatoes, and garlic in a 5-quart soup kettle and add water to cover by 2 inches. Simmer gently, stirring from time to time, for 1½ hours. Add the mushrooms and potatoes and cook for 30 minutes longer or until meat is fork tender and barley and beans are cooked through. Taste for seasoning, add pepper and salt to taste, and serve.

YIELD: *8 to 12 servings.*

*Advice from Mama:* This soup gets even better the next day and the next. Simply add a little water each time (remember about that barley!) and reheat.

## 3

# EGG DISHES

□ □ □ □ □ □ □ □ □ □ □ □ □ □ □ □ □ □ □ □ □ □ □ □ □ □ □ □ □ □ □

I *hate the word* "cholesterol" whenever these recipes come up because every single one of these dishes is delicious and can be eaten with gusto almost every day. When I was growing up, eggs were not only considered to be good for you, but they were "nature's perfect food."

One of my favorite memories of childhood is when my aunt Dora used to send us a large crate of freshly laid eggs from the country. In those days we had to eat at least one egg a day, and more was better. Since I would only eat my eggs well done, my mother made my egg in a special way. She cut a hole in a piece of bread, melted some butter in a pan, put the bread in the sizzling butter, and the egg went into the hole in the bread. This was fried until it was nice and crispy on one side, turned over and fried to a crispy finish on the other. Delicious? You bet! Cholesterol? No kidding!

Some of my readers may remember when their mothers or

grandmothers could go and buy a fresh-killed chicken or pullet. Sometimes these chickens still had a few tiny, soft, not-yet-laid eggs (*ayeleh*, in Yiddish) hidden inside. Perhaps their mothers, like my mother, never wasted anything and these unlaid eggs were added as a special treat to enrich the chicken soup. I remember how my sisters and I squabbled over who got more or the biggest of these special delicacies. Several times over the past years I've gone out of the way to find and buy freshly killed chickens in order to let my children experience this treat. I recommend it to all my readers.

Now I'm not telling you to cook all the egg dishes in this chapter every day, but as far as I'm concerned, life without an occasional Sunday-morning dish of salami and eggs, matzo brei, or French toast made from challah is not worth living. So, remember, everything in moderation is okay. Anyway, that's what my doctor keeps telling me, in the same breath that he's telling me that I've got to lose weight.

# Lox with Eggs and Onion

If you were brought up in an old-fashioned Jewish household, you know that when you can't afford to buy a lot of lox for Sunday breakfast or brunch, you buy a little bit and figure out a way to make it go around. If you make lox with eggs and onion, you won't suffer and you won't feel poor. This is, in fact, one of the most popular breakfast dishes that I served in my restaurant. Of course, since I felt that most of my customers were like family, I didn't skimp on the amount of lox I added to this recipe.

*4 tablespoons butter or margarine*
*1 large onion, diced*
*¼ pound lox or Nova Scotia*

*smoked salmon, coarsely chopped*
*10 large eggs, beaten*

Heat the butter or margarine in a large skillet. Sauté the onion until it turns golden brown. Add the smoked salmon and the eggs and cook, stirring, until eggs are scrambled to your taste. If you prefer, cook without stirring until eggs are set, turn with a spatula, and cook pancake style. Serve immediately with hot toasted bagels.

YIELD:   *4 servings.*


# Mama Leah's Jewish Western Omelet

Since my restaurant served only Jewish-American food (not kosher), I didn't have any pork or shellfish. But since I, personally, love a Western omelet, I devised this recipe and it proved to be a favorite.

*4 tablespoons butter or*
   *margarine*
*1 large onion, diced*
*1 medium green bell pepper,*
   *cored and diced*

*8 to 10 mushrooms, sliced*
*1 tomato, diced*
*¼ pound lox or Nova Scotia*
   *smoked salmon*
*10 large eggs*

Heat the butter or margarine in a large skillet. Sauté the onion until golden brown. Add the green pepper and mushrooms and sauté for a few minutes longer, until vegetables wilt and soften. Add the tomato, smoked salmon, and eggs. Cook, stirring, until eggs are scrambled and cooked to your taste. If you prefer, cook without stirring until eggs are set, turn with a spatula, and cook pancake style.

YIELD:   *4 servings.*

*Advice from Mama:*   This is a wonderful breakfast or brunch meal, and it goes great with bagels and cream cheese or butter. If you plan on having a larger group of people over for brunch, you can double the recipe. Preheat your oven to 350°F. Separate the eggs and mix the omelet ingredients with the yolks. Beat the egg whites until stiff and fold into the mixture. Pour into a greased baking pan (measuring approximately 9 by 12 inches) and bake for 20 to 25 minutes, until the eggs have set and look fluffy and golden on top. Cut into rectangular pieces in the pan and serve with a spatula. Good at room temperature, too.

# Salami and Eggs

I remember my father coming home from work one day with a long, well-wrapped package under his arm. Because he spoiled me more than my sisters I was sure it was something for me. "Papa," I said, "did you bring me home a present?" "No," he answered with a sly smile. "These are just my tools." But when my sisters and I discovered this package hanging behind the kitchen door, curiosity got the better of us and we unwrapped the package to find a big, fat kosher salami. Naturally we tucked right in and devoured most of it. When my father walked into the kitchen, we all three looked up at him and said, "Papa, those were the best tools we ever ate!" He got such a kick out of it, he just laughed, and even years later would grin when we reminded him of those delicious "tools." Fortunately we saved just enough to still have salami and eggs for supper.

*12 slices kosher beef salami*     *1 tablespoon corn oil,*
  *(slices approximately ¼ inch*       *margarine, or butter*
  *thick)*                        *6 eggs*

Cut each salami slice into halves, or smaller if you prefer, and sauté in corn oil, margarine, or butter over medium heat, until slightly crisp. Turn salami pieces with a spatula and crisp on other side. Beat the eggs and pour over the salami. When cooked on bottom side, turn over with a large spatula, or cut in half and turn each half over, to cook on other side. Eggs should be cooked firm and well done. If you prefer your eggs soft, let the eggs set on one side only and do not turn. Serve with either ketchup or mustard.

YIELD: *2 servings.*

*Advice from Mama:* This makes a great Sunday-morning breakfast served with lots of orange juice, hot coffee, and fresh toasted bagels or toasted rye bread. When I was a child my mother used to serve salami and eggs accompanied by Heinz vegetarian baked beans for a quick economical dinner, and I still do it when I find I have to feed an unexpected guest or two. My mother liked to serve a piece of melon first, and for dessert there was coffee cake or rugalach. What more could any person want?

# Challah French Toast

By Sunday morning the challah you baked on Friday is perfect for making French toast. Sure, you could use fresh challah from the bakery and it will be almost as good, and, believe me, that's plenty good enough. French toast made with bread other than challah, why waste the calories?

| | |
|---|---|
| *6 eggs* | *¹/₄ teaspoon salt* |
| *¹/₂ cup heavy cream,* | *4 to 6 tablespoons clarified* |
| *half-and-half, or milk* | *butter* |
| *1 teaspoon cinnamon* | *8 slices challah, cut 1 inch thick* |

Beat the eggs together with cream, half-and-half, or milk. Beat in cinnamon and salt. Melt the butter in a large frying pan. Dip the challah slices, one at a time, into the egg mixture, making sure that each slice is well coated. The challah should absorb a little of the egg mixture but not enough to get soggy. Fry each battered challah slice for 2 to 3 minutes on one side until it turns golden brown, and the same on the other side. Don't fry too fast or the inside will be wet and gooey.

Serve with your favorite jam, maple syrup, honey, cinnamon sugar, or plain, which is the way I like it best.

YIELD: *4 to 8 servings.*

*Advice from Mama:* Heavy cream really is the best liquid to use in this recipe. It makes the egg batter in the challah puff up to a gorgeous golden brown when you fry it in hot butter.

# 4

# GRAINS *and* NOODLES

□ □ □ □ □ □ □ □ □ □ □ □ □ □ □ □ □ □ □ □ □ □ □ □ □ □ □

T*he Russian people* have an old folk saying that goes, "Schi and kasha are our food." Schi is a cabbage soup eaten by peasants all winter long, and kasha, in Russian, refers to any cereal grain cooked into a porridge. It seems a meager diet to us now, although all our doctors would be much happier if we ate much more cabbage and grains than most other things. Cabbage, we now know, not only fills the belly but provides fiber, vitamins and minerals, and protects us from certain kinds of cancer. Grains, whether they be nutty, nutritious buckwheat groats, lovely, comforting rice, or ordinary wheat flour transformed into golden, delicious noodles, are the perfect complex carbohydrates, also providing that all-important fiber and lots of good energy to deal with our complex world.

We used to think that starches, like grains, noodles, and beans, were fattening, in the sense that they were filled with empty calories and not much else. Now we find that they're called "complex carbohydrates" and that they're very good for you. And all along the peasants and poor Jews of Eastern Europe survived and thrived on diets of kasha, noodles, beans, cabbage, carrots, beets, and onions. And everything eaten with a hunk of heavy black bread.

# Noodles with Cottage Cheese and Butter (Lukschen Kase mit Putter)

This delicious Jewish version of fettuccine Alfredo was another one of my mother's standbys for a good economical lunch or dinner on a hot summer's day. Whenever my niece, Debbie, spoke to my mother from anywhere in the country, she would say, "Grandma, when I come home, will you make me your lukschen kase mit putter?" Do you think my mother said no to her grandchild? Which reminds me of how Sam Levenson used to say that the reason grandparents and grandchildren get along so well is that they have a common enemy.

*1 pound egg noodles, medium wide*
*1 pint dry cottage cheese or pot cheese*
*6 tablespoons butter, softened to room temperature*
*1 teaspoon salt*
*1/8 teaspoon white pepper*

Bring a large pot of lightly salted water to a boil. Cook the noodles until tender. Drain and replace in pot over very low heat. Add the cheese, butter, salt, and pepper. Toss everything together until cheese starts to melt. Serve immediately with a green tossed salad.

YIELD: *4 to 6 servings.*

# Lukschen Kugel (Milchig)

There's a Jewish saying that goes: If a woman can't make a kugel—divorce her! This may seem a bit overly strict, but it does make clear how strongly some people feel about kugel—many are convinced that it is simply the best thing that can be done with noodles (lukschen). Traditionally a kugel is associated with holidays, particularly Chanukah, and with the Sabbath. It can be prepared the night before and kept in a warm oven or served at room temperature.

Many people have begged me for my lukschen kugel recipe, which I have never given out, but I did always promise that if and when I ever wrote a cookbook, I would put it in. So here's my secret special kugel . . . guaranteed protection against divorce!

*1 pound medium egg noodles*
*6 medium eggs*
*1 1/2 cups milk*
*1 cup cottage cheese or pot cheese*
*1 cup sour cream*
*1/2 cup sugar*
*1 cup raisins (optional)*
*1/2 cup brown sugar*
*1/2 cup chopped walnuts or pecans*
*1 tablespoon cinnamon*

Preheat oven to 350°F.

Bring a large pot of lightly salted water to a boil. Cook the noodles until just tender, then drain. While noodles are cooking, beat the eggs in a large bowl. Add milk, cheese, sour cream, white sugar, and raisins. Beat together and then add noodles. Mix well. Pour into a buttered 10-by-14-inch pan. Mix together the brown sugar, nuts, and cinnamon. Sprinkle evenly over the noodles and bake for 1 hour or until center seems to be firm.

Cool and serve warm or at room temperature.

YIELD: *10 to 14 pieces.*

*Advice from Mama:*

*1.* A kugel is great for a snack or dessert. It reheats perfectly to make a great breakfast (and it's not bad cold with a glass of milk). And if you serve it as part of a buffet table at a party, it'll disappear in no time at all.

2. To freeze for a future occasion: Bake the kugel for 45 minutes, let cool, wrap well, and freeze. When ready to use, bake at 350°F for another 45 minutes and serve.

# Dried Fruit Noodle Kugel

Dried fruit noodle kugel can be served as a dessert or just a nosh. Have it with a cup of tea or coffee for a nice midafternoon pick-me-up. I even like it for breakfast. It is especially good for a buffet party because it can be served hot, warm, or at room temperature.

*1/2 cup raisins*
*1 cup pitted prunes*
*1/2 cup dried apricots*
*16 ounces egg noodles, medium
  width*
*1/2 cup melted butter or
  margarine*

*6 eggs*
*3 tablespoons brown sugar*
*Juice of 1 lemon*
*1/4 cup brown sugar*
*1/4 cup chopped walnuts or
  pecans*
*1 teaspoon cinnamon*

Soak the raisins, prunes, and apricots in water to cover overnight or cook in water to cover until fruits are soft, about 30 minutes.

Preheat oven to 350°F.

Drain fruits and set aside. Cook the noodles in a large pot of lightly salted boiling water according to package directions. Do not overcook the noodles, they will continue cooking in the oven. Drain and put them in a large mixing bowl. Toss with melted butter or margarine and let cool slightly. Beat the eggs together with the 3 tablespoons of brown sugar and the lemon juice. Add to noodles, together with soaked dried fruit and mix well. Place in a well-greased ovenproof casserole. In a small bowl mix together the remaining brown sugar, chopped nuts, and cinnamon. Sprinkle over the noodles and bake for 45 to 60 minutes, until well browned.

YIELD: *8 to 10 servings.*

# Lukschen Kugel (Flaischig)

The famous German-Jewish poet Heinrich Heine referred to kugel as "this national holy dish." What more can I say?

This kugel is delicious served as a side dish with pot roast or brisket.

*1 pound egg noodles, medium width*
*6 eggs*
*2 teaspoons salt*

*1 teaspoon white pepper*
*1 large onion, diced fine*
*½ cup Schmaltz (rendered chicken fat) (page 10)*

Bring a large pot of lightly salted water to the boil and cook the noodles until they are just tender. Drain, cool slightly under cold running water, and place them in a large bowl. Beat the eggs together with the salt and pepper, add them to the noodles, and mix well.

Preheat oven to 375°F.

Brown the onion in the schmaltz, let cool slightly, and stir into noodle-egg mixture. Grease an ovenproof 10-by-14-inch pan with either chicken fat or oil and arrange the noodle mixture in it. Bake for 45 minutes or until the noodles start to brown.

YIELD: *6 to 10 servings.*

*Advice from Mama:* The only ingredient making this dish "fleischig" is the schmaltz. If you substitute corn oil for the schmaltz, the dish will be "parve" and can be served as part of a dairy or vegetarian meal.

# Kasha

When I lived at home before I married, I just hated kasha. My reaction each time my mother said she was making kasha, was a verbal "Eech!" When I had been married for about a year, I suddenly developed an urge for kasha. After several disastrous attempts, I finally mastered the knack of preparing delicious kasha. Then we started to have it so often that my late husband, Stan, would say, "Enough already!"

I think it goes particularly well with pot roast, brisket, and fricassee. If you have any leftover kasha, you can put it in chicken soup.

All over Poland, Russia, and the Ukraine kasha is often served as a breakfast cereal because it's widely available and extremely nourishing. If you want to try it, cook it with extra water and serve with milk and brown sugar or honey.

1 cup medium buckwheat groats
(coarse or fine may be used
also)
1 egg
2 cups boiling chicken stock or 1
Knorr chicken bouillon cube
dissolved in 2 cups water

or

2 cups boiling water
1 1/2 teaspoons salt (less if
bouillon cube is used)

In a small bowl mix groats with egg until each groat is well coated with egg. Place in medium-size saucepan over moderately high heat. Stir constantly with a wooden spoon until groats separate and the egg begins to dry. Be careful not to burn the groats.

Remove from heat and pour boiling chicken stock or water over kasha. Add salt and stir. Cover tightly and cook over low heat at a bare simmer for 10 minutes, or until all the liquid is absorbed.

YIELD: *4 servings.*

*Advice from Mama:* If you wish to try the unroasted buckwheat that is sold in health food stores, you can roast it yourself in a preheated 350°F oven. Spread the buckwheat groats on a cookie sheet and roast for 15 to 20 minutes, until the groats start to turn golden brown. Remove from oven and proceed with recipe above.

# Kasha and Mushrooms

Whenever I make kasha this way, I always try to make a little more than I need because I know I'm going to nosh at least one serving.

1 cup medium buckwheat groats (whole, coarse, or fine may be used also)
1 egg
2 cups boiling chicken stock or 1 Knorr chicken bouillon cube dissolved in 2 cups water
or

2 cups boiling water
1½ teaspoons salt (less if bouillon cube is used)
¼ cup corn oil
1 large onion, chopped
10 to 12 large mushrooms, sliced
Salt to taste

In a small bowl mix groats with egg until each groat is well coated with egg. Place in medium-size saucepan, over moderately high heat, and stir constantly with a wooden spoon until groats separate and the egg begins to dry.

Remove from heat and pour boiling chicken stock or water over kasha. Add salt and stir. Cover tightly and cook over low heat at a bare simmer for 10 to 15 minutes, or until all the liquid is absorbed. Remove from heat and reserve.

Heat the oil in a large skillet and sauté the onions until golden brown. Add the mushrooms and cook, stirring until mushrooms wilt and soften. Drain the cooked onions and mushrooms in a sieve to remove excess oil. Add the onion-mushroom mixture to the cooked kasha. Mix well and add salt if necessary.

YIELD: *4 to 6 servings.*

*Advice from Mama:* If you prefer a purely vegetarian dish, substitute vegetable broth or water for the chicken broth. Even made with plain water it still tastes yummy because of the sautéed onions.

# Kasha Varnishkes

This is a classic Jewish dish, and if you don't know it, it deserves to be introduced to you.

*1 cup medium buckwheat groats (whole, coarse, or fine may be used also)*
*1 egg*
*2 cups boiling chicken stock or 1 Knorr chicken bouillon cube dissolved in 2 cups water*
*or*
*2 cups boiling water*
*1 1/2 teaspoons salt (less if bouillon cube is used)*

*1 quart water*
*1 cup uncooked varnishkes (bowtie noodles or broad egg noodles broken into pieces approximately the size of a bowtie noodle)*
*3 tablespoons corn oil*
*1 large onion, coarsley chopped*

In a small bowl mix groats with egg until each groat is well coated with egg. Place in medium-size saucepan over moderately high heat, and stir constantly with a wooden spoon until groats separate and the egg begins to dry.

Remove from heat and pour boiling chicken stock or water over kasha. Add salt and stir. Cover tightly and cook over low heat at a bare simmer for 10 to 15 minutes, or until all the liquid is absorbed. Remove from heat and reserve.

Bring the quart of water to a boil and cook the pasta about 15 minutes, until tender. Drain and reserve.

Heat the oil in a skillet and sauté the onions until golden brown. Mix the onions, kasha, and cooked bowties together in a large bowl and serve. Serve with pot roast or just with leftover pot roast gravy. Good all by itself, too.

YIELD:   *6 servings.*

*Advice from Mama:*   For a more delicious and authentic version, substitute ¼ cup schmaltz for the corn oil.

# Mushrooms and Egg Barley

Egg barley or farfel is now sold in packages in most grocery stores, my favorite brand being the one made by Goodman. It comes toasted and plain, but the toasted has a nice nutty flavor that most people really enjoy. If you can't find toasted egg barley, use the plain, or toast it yourself—spread on a baking sheet in a 350°F oven for 20 minutes.

Farfel is the Jewish contribution to the huge world of pasta. When it was made at home, back in the old country, it was made from noodle dough that was cut into small bits, which were then dried and toasted. In some parts of Europe farfel was made from leftover bits of bread dough, insuring that nothing was wasted.

Some Jews see a hopeful symbolism in the roundness of the farfel pellets and like to eat them for the New Year, in the hopes that their sins will be forgiven and prosperity will follow.

I like to eat farfel anytime because it is so delicious. This dish makes a good nosh by itself or it can be served as a side dish instead of potatoes, rice, or noodles.

| | |
|---|---|
| *8 cups water* | *½ pound mushrooms, sliced* |
| *1 tablespoon salt* | *4 tablespoons corn oil* |
| *2 cups toasted egg barley* | *1 teaspoon salt or to taste* |
| *2 large onions, finely chopped* | *½ teaspoon garlic powder* |

Bring the 8 cups of water and 1 tablespoon of salt to a boil. Add the egg barley and cook for approximately 20 minutes, until they are tender. Meanwhile sauté the onions and mushrooms in corn oil until the onions have browned. Drain the cooked onions and mushrooms in a sieve to remove excess oil.

Drain the egg barley and place in a bowl. Mix together with the onions and mushrooms, salt and garlic powder, and serve.

YIELD: *8 to 10 servings.*

# Mamaliga

Mamaliga, a porridge or mush made from cornmeal (very similar to Italian polenta and American hasty pudding), was Columbus's gift to the hungry Jews of Romania and the rest of Southeastern Europe, where the corn kernels brought back from the New World grew and thrived. Mamaliga—the word is derived from the Venetian *meliga*—can be plain or fancy, but it is always satisfying and filling.

*6 cups water*
*2 cups cornmeal*
*1 teaspoon kosher salt*
*3 tablespoons butter or margarine*

*2 pounds farmer cheese or dry cottage cheese*
*1/4 teaspoon salt*
*1/4 teaspoon pepper*

Mix 1 cup cold water into the cornmeal, stirring well to prevent lumps. Place remaining 5 cups water in the top of a double boiler over moderate heat. Slowly stir in the moistened cornmeal and continue stirring for 8 to 10 minutes. Add salt and butter or margarine and mix well. Cover and continue cooking for 20 to 25 minutes, until thickened to desired consistency. Some people say it should be thick enough for a wooden spoon to stand up in it. Turn the mamaliga out on a large platter and make a well in the center.

Mix farmer or cottage cheese with salt and pepper and place in the center of the mamaliga. This is very nice served with Fried Herring (page 125).

YIELD: *6 to 8 servings.*

*Advice from Mama:* Cold leftover mamaliga can be sliced and fried in butter or margarine for breakfast, a snack, or to go with any dish that has good gravy to soak up.

# Rice Pilaf

I make this rice dish very often because it goes so well with so many different dishes, especially lamb, chicken, and fish.

*1 ½ cups long-grain white rice*
*2 tablespoons butter or*
   *margarine*

*1 Knorr chicken bouillon cube*
*3 cups boiling water*

In a heavy saucepan or a skillet with a tight-fitting lid, sauté the rice in butter or margarine over medium heat, stirring constantly, until rice begins to brown (5 to 8 minutes). Dissolve the bouillon cube in hot water. Add water to the rice, stir once, and cover the pot. Reduce heat to lowest setting and cook for 20 minutes or until all the liquid is absorbed.

YIELD: *6 to 8 servings.*

*Advice from Mama:* You can just as easily make this pilaf with brown rice. Just increase the cooking time to 40 minutes.

# Beans and Brown Rice

This recipe is not handed down from my or anybody else's *bubba*. I developed it for some of my non-meat-eating customers. It is delicious, healthful, and an excellent source of complex carbohydrates, which is what we're all supposed to be eating more of these days.

<sup></sup>

| | |
|---|---|
| ½ cup dried beans (navy, kidney, chick-peas, or any other bean of your choice) | 1 cup brown rice |
| | 2 cups boiling water |
| | 1 Knorr chicken bouillon cube |
| 2 tablespoons corn oil, butter, or Schmaltz (rendered chicken fat) (page 10) | Salt to taste |
| | ¼ teaspoon freshly ground black pepper |
| 1 medium onion, finely diced | |

Soak beans in cold water overnight. Drain the beans, place them in a pot with 3 cups water and simmer for 1½ hours. Remove from heat and drain the beans.

Heat the oil, butter, or schmaltz in the bottom of a heavy pot or Dutch oven. Add the onion and sauté for about 5 minutes, until wilted. Stir in rice and cook, stirring for a few minutes until rice is coated with oil. Add the boiling water, beans, and bouillon cube. Stir, reduce heat to very low, cover the pot tightly, and cook for 45 to 60 minutes, until all the water is absorbed and beans and rice are tender. Check for seasoning and add salt and pepper if desired.

YIELD: *6 servings.*

*Advice from Mama:*

1. You can add diced green pepper and/or crushed tomatoes to dress up this dish. Sauté with the onion and proceed as described above.
2. If you are pressed for time, substitute 1 cup canned beans for the dried beans. Rinse under cold running water and add to rice as described above.

# Rice and Peas

I love this dish with fish, and it's also great for those times when you don't feel like potatoes or noodles.

*2 tablespoons butter or*
  *margarine*
*1 onion, minced*
*1 cup long-grain white rice*

*2 cups boiling water*
*2 teaspoons salt*
*1 package frozen peas, defrosted*

Heat the butter or margarine in the bottom of a heavy saucepan with a tight-fitting lid. Sauté the onion for about 5 minutes, then add the rice and sauté, stirring, for 1 minute more. Add the water and salt, stir, reduce heat to a low simmer and cover tightly. Cook for 20 to 25 minutes, until rice is tender and most of the water is absorbed. Stir in peas, cover, and cook 5 minutes longer.

Y I E L D :   *4 to 6 servings.*

# 5

# BLINTZES, KNISHES, LATKES, VARENIKIS, *and* OTHER GOODIES

□ □ □ □ □ □ □ □ □ □ □ □ □ □ □ □ □ □ □ □ □ □ □ □ □ □ □ □ □ □ □ □ □ □ □ □ □ □ □ □

*he blintzes, knishes,* chremslach, latkes, and varenikis in this section represent what I consider to be the glories of Jewish cooking. Not one of the items in this section can be eaten by people on a slimming diet. They are all gloriously fattening, usually made more so by side dishes of melted butter, sour cream, preserves, etc. Nevertheless, if you have eaten any of these foods in your childhood, there will come a day when you have an irresistible longing to eat them again. And then, for a short time, let all the diets be damned, *Ess kinderlach!* And enjoy!

Blintzes are related etymologically to Russian blinis, but culinarily they are much closer to French crepes. Russian blinis are yeast-raised pancakes, often made with buckwheat flour, and are traditionally served during Lent. This tradition goes back to pre-Christian times, when blinis were eaten to celebrate the coming of the spring equinox, because the round shape of the blinis suggested the roundness of the sun. Blintzes, much thinner, crepe-like pancakes, are also round before they are wrapped around a delicious filling, but are eaten all year round. Cheese blintzes are particularly associated with the festival of Shevuot, when it is customary to eat only dairy dishes.

Are knishes a dumpling or a pastry? I vote for pastry, but I've seen them called dumplings, too. All I know is that knishes are a little bit of delicious filling with some dough wrapped around. Anyway, who cares what you call them as long as you can get to eat some.

Latkes are pancakes, but usually a very special kind of pancake made from potatoes. They used to be really hard to make because the potatoes had to be grated by hand, but today what do we have a food processor for, anyway? To make latkes, of course.

Chremslach are a kind of Jewish fritter, and varenikis are, in fact, delicious dumplings filled with fruit, cheese, or savory mashed potatoes. But enough definitions. Get into the kitchen and make something. My mouth is watering.

## Blintzes

Blintzes exist in two stages. First, there is the crepe (a very thin pancake), which can be made way ahead to have on hand for making blintzes. Then there is the blintze, once the crepe has been stuffed and rolled into its final shape. In this section I give nine separate filling recipes, but these should only be a starting point for you. Blintze fillings are the perfect medium for improvisation, and you should certainly experiment and try coming up with some of your own. Do you have any interesting leftovers in your refrigerator? Chop them up small or puree them and use as a filling for blintzes. I know a man who always makes blintzes from leftover Chinese food! So be creative and let your imagination run wild. But first try my blintze fillings to get an idea of what blintzes can be.

Making your own blintzes may seem complicated, but they are

really among the easiest dishes to make and they can be prepared three or four days in advance and reheated for a quick meal. In fact, you can have them all prepared and ready to cook anytime in your freezer.

The knack of making perfectly shaped thin crepes (*blet lach,* in Yiddish, meaning "leaves") takes a little practice to perfect—it's all in the quick wrist action. But even if they're not perfect, they're still delicious, and before you know it, you'll be using two frying pans at once and speeding up the time and quantity.

After you make the crepes, choose your filling. Place a heaping tablespoon of filling in the middle of the crepe. Fold the bottom of the crepe up over the filling. Fold opposite sides of the crepe in to meet in the middle. Now fold crepe over again to completely enclose the filling. Arrange filled crepes, fold side down on a platter, to wait until all the blintzes are made. Now you can cook the blintzes and refrigerate or freeze them for later.

If you plan on making a lot of blintzes for a party, here is a good tip. Sauté the blintzes very quickly and place them on a baking sheet. Cover and refrigerate. You can do this days or hours before your company arrives. About 20 minutes before serving, place the blintzes on a baking sheet and put into an oven preheated to 375°F. Bake for 20 minutes. Transfer the hot blintzes to a serving platter and enjoy your extra free time.

### Batter

| | |
|---|---|
| *4 eggs* | *1 cup all-purpose flour* |
| *1 tablespoon corn oil* | *Pinch of salt (optional)* |
| *1 cup milk or water* | |

Combine eggs and oil in a bowl and beat until light and frothy. Beat in milk or water, then beat in flour and optional salt. Beat until well blended. Pour the batter into a pitcher, cover, and refrigerate for 10 to 15 minutes, until flour absorbs liquid and thickens.

Place an 8- or 9-inch frying pan or omelet pan (if you have the nonstick kind, this is the time to use it) over medium heat. Dip a piece of paper towel in some vegetable oil and lightly grease the frying pan. When it is very hot, quickly pour some batter into the skillet, swirl very quickly to cover entire surface, and rapidly pour back excess into pitcher. When the batter starts curling away from sides of pan it is done. Shake it out onto a clean dish towel or paper towels. Repeat until all the crepes are done. Cover with plastic wrap or a damp dish towel until you are ready to use them to prevent the crepes from drying out.

YIELD: *16–18 crepes.*

*To freeze the crepes:* Crepes freeze perfectly at this point and you can always have them on hand to make up a batch of blintzes. Place a piece of waxed paper between each layer of crepes and arrange them in a stack of about 16 crepes. Wrap them very well in heavy-duty aluminum foil or place them in an airtight plastic container. When you want to make blintzes, remove as many of the frozen crepes as you will need and leave them out at room temperature. They will defrost in 20 to 30 minutes.

Most filled blintzes may be frozen before cooking as well. The only ones I don't like to freeze are the cheese blintzes, because freezing changes the texture of the cheese, but not the taste. Let frozen blintzes defrost completely, then fry in butter or margarine until golden brown.

Blintzes can even be frozen after they are fried. Defrost them completely and reheat in a 325°F oven for 20 minutes.

# Blintzes with Cheese Filling

*½ pound farmer cheese (if farmer cheese is not available, use large-curd cottage cheese)*

*1 pint pot cheese or cottage cheese*

*1 to 2 tablespoons sugar (as you like it)*

*2 tablespoons sour cream*

*16 to 18 prepared crepes for blintzes (page 98)*

*2 to 4 tablespoons butter or margarine for frying*

Blend cheese, sugar, and sour cream together until creamy. Place a heaping tablespoon of filling in the middle of a crepe. Fold the bottom of the crepe up over the filling. Fold opposite sides of the crepe in to meet in the middle. Now fold crepe over again to completely enclose the filling. Arrange filled crepes, fold side down, on a platter to wait until all the blintzes are made. (When blintzes are filled they can be frozen or refrigerated until ready to use.)

Melt 2 tablespoons butter or margarine in a frying pan and fry on both sides, over moderate heat, until golden brown. Add more butter or margarine to the frying pan as necessary.

Serve hot with sour cream and/or blueberry jam.

YIELD: *16 to 18 blintzes.*

# Blintzes "Litvak" Style

I call these blintzes "Litvak" style because Lithuanians don't care for a sweet blintze. The Litvaks from Vilna, like my father, thought this was the only true and proper way to make blintzes. In fact, Litvaks tended to think that anything from Vilna was superior to anything from anywhere else. In some cases they were right, but don't tell my "Galitzianer" (Jews from Galicia, a province of Poland/Austria) friends.

*1 to 1½ pounds farmer cheese (if farmer cheese is not available, use large-curd cottage cheese)*
*2 tablespoons sour cream*
*1 egg*

*½ teaspoon salt*
*½ teaspoon white pepper*
*16 to 18 prepared crepes for blintzes (page 98)*
*2 to 4 tablespoons butter or margarine for frying*

Blend cheese, sour cream, egg, salt, and pepper together until creamy. Place a heaping tablespoon of filling in the middle of a crepe. Fold the bottom of the crepe up over the filling. Fold opposite sides of the crepe in to meet in the middle. Now fold crepe over again to completely enclose the filling. Arrange filled crepes, fold side down, on a platter to wait until all the blintzes are made. (When blintzes are filled they can be frozen or refrigerated until ready to use.)

Melt 2 tablespoons butter or margarine in a frying pan and fry on both sides until golden brown. Add more butter or margarine to the frying pan as necessary.

Serve hot with sour cream.

YIELD:   *16 to 18 blintzes.*

# Blintzes with Kasha Filling
—————————————— ❧ ——————————————

*1 cup kasha (buckwheat groats)*
*About 4 cups boiling water*
*2 teaspoons salt*
*2 tablespoons corn oil*
*1 onion, diced*
*¼ pound mushrooms, sliced*

*Freshly ground black pepper*
  *(optional)*
*16 to 18 prepared crepes for*
  *blintzes (page 98)*
*2 to 4 tablespoons butter or*
  *margarine for frying*

Place kasha in a heavy saucepan and pour boiling water over it until kasha is just covered. Add salt, stir, cover saucepan, and cook over very low heat until kasha has absorbed all the water and is cooked (about 20 minutes).

Heat the oil in a skillet and sauté the onion until just golden brown. Add the sliced mushrooms and sauté for a few minutes longer until mushrooms are just done. Season with freshly ground black pepper to taste and stir into cooked kasha. Cool to room temperature before filling blintzes. Place about 1 tablespoon of filling in the center of a crepe. Fold the bottom of the crepe up over the filling. Fold opposite sides of the crepe in to meet in the middle. Now fold crepe over again to completely enclose the filling. Arrange filled crepes, fold side down, on a platter to wait until all the blintzes are made. (When blintzes are filled they can be frozen or refrigerated until ready to use.)

Melt 2 tablespoons butter or margarine in a frying pan and fry on both sides until golden brown. Add more butter or margarine to the frying pan as necessary.

Serve plain or with sour cream or a gravy from your brisket or pot roast.

YIELD:   *16 to 18 blintzes.*

# Blintzes with Meat Filling

2 tablespoons vegetable oil
1 medium onion, chopped fine
1 medium green pepper, diced
   fine
8 medium mushrooms, sliced
   thin
2 cloves garlic, crushed
1 teaspoon salt
1/4 teaspoon freshly ground
   black pepper

2 tablespoons ketchup
1 1/2 pounds ground round or
   chuck
16 to 18 prepared crepes for
   blintzes (page 98)
2 to 4 tablespoons butter or
   margarine for frying

Heat the oil in a heavy skillet and sauté the onion and pepper until they are soft. Add the mushrooms, garlic, salt, pepper, and ketchup, sauté for another minute, stirring continuously. Add the ground meat and cook, stirring, until meat has lost all traces of pink color. Remove from heat and place meat mixture into a large sieve over a bowl to drain off excess oil and rendered fat. Allow to cool before filling crepes. Place about 1 tablespoon of filling in the center of each crepe. Fold the bottom of the crepe up over the filling. Fold opposite sides of the crepe in to meet in the middle. Now fold crepe over again to completely enclose the filling. Arrange filled crepes, fold side down, on a platter to wait until all the blintzes are made. (When blintzes are filled they can be frozen or refrigerated until ready to use.)

Melt 2 tablespoons butter or margarine in a frying pan and fry on both sides until golden brown. Add more butter or margarine to the frying pan as necessary. Serve hot.

YIELD: *16 to 18 blintzes.*

## Blintzes with Potato Filling

*3 large russet or Idaho potatoes*
*1 large onion, diced*
*3 tablespoons corn oil*
*1 tablespoon salt or to taste*
*1 teaspoon freshly ground black pepper or to taste*

*16 to 18 prepared crepes for blintzes (page 98)*
*2 to 4 tablespoons butter or margarine for frying*

Peel the potatoes, slice thin, and boil them in salted water to cover until they are tender. While they are cooking, sauté the onion in corn oil until it is a dark golden brown. Drain the potatoes and place them in a bowl. Mash them together with the sautéed onions. Season with salt and freshly ground black pepper to taste. Place about 1 tablespoon filling in the center of a crepe. Fold the bottom of the crepe up over the filling. Fold opposite sides of the crepe in to meet in the middle. Now fold crepe over again to completely enclose the filling. Arrange filled crepes, fold side down, on a platter to wait until all the blintzes are made. (When blintzes are filled they can be frozen or refrigerated until ready to use.)

Melt 2 tablespoons butter or margarine in a frying pan and fry on both sides until golden brown. Add more butter or margarine to the frying pan as necessary.

Serve with sour cream or yogurt.

YIELD: *16 to 18 blintzes.*

# Blintzes Filled with Shredded Vegetables

2 stalks celery, no leaves
1 medium onion, peeled
2 large carrots
2 small zucchini
2 stalks broccoli
1 small chicken bouillon cube
1 tablespoon soy sauce
2 tablespoons corn or sunflower oil

1 clove garlic, crushed
¼ cup water
16 to 18 prepared crepes for blintzes (page 98)
2 to 4 tablespoons butter or margarine for frying

Cut celery in the Chinese style by cutting thin slices on the diagonal. Cut onion in half and slice thin. Cut carrots and zucchini in diagonal slices and then slice into julienne pieces. Cut broccoli into small pieces.

Parboil carrots for 5 minutes, then add onion, celery, broccoli, and zucchini for an additional 3 minutes. Drain and set aside. Mash bouillon cube into soy sauce with a wooden spoon to dissolve. Heat the oil in a large sauté pan, add garlic, soy sauce, mashed bouillon cube, and water. Cook over low heat, stirring, for about 1 minute. Add all the vegetables and cook, stirring, until vegetables are well coated and cooked through. Let cool before filling crepes. Place about 1 tablespoon filling in the center of a crepe. Fold the bottom of the crepe up over the filling. Fold opposite sides of the crepe in to meet in the middle. Now fold crepe over again to completely enclose the filling. Arrange filled crepes, fold side down, on a platter to wait until all the blintzes are made. (When blintzes are filled they can be frozen or refrigerated until ready to use.)

Melt 2 tablespoons butter or margarine in a frying pan and fry on both sides until golden brown. Add more butter or margarine to the frying pan as necessary.

Serve vegetable-filled blintzes plain or with yogurt.

YIELD: *16 to 18 blintzes.*

# Blintzes Reuben's Style

This recipe is a good example of how you can be creative and imaginative with blintzes. One day, while enjoying a fine Reuben sandwich, I realized that the same filling might work inside a blintze. I tried it and it has been a huge success. Don't forget to serve Russian dressing on the side.

*1 pound sliced corned beef or pastrami*
*½ pound sliced Swiss cheese*
*1 teaspoon caraway seeds (optional)*
*½ pound fresh, canned, or packaged sauerkraut, rinsed and drained*

*16 to 18 prepared crepes for blintzes (page 98)*
*1 cup Russian dressing (see page 107)*
*2 to 4 tablespoons butter or margarine for frying*

Cut sliced corned beef into thin strips. Do the same with the Swiss cheese. If you like, add caraway seeds to sauerkraut and mix well. Place some corned beef in center of crepe, add some cheese, then top with sauerkraut. Fold the bottom of the crepe up over the filling. Fold opposite sides of the crepe in to meet in the middle. Now fold crepe over again to completely enclose the filling. Arrange filled crepes, fold side down, on a platter to wait until all the blintzes are made. (When blintzes are filled they can be frozen or refrigerated until ready to use.)

Melt 2 tablespoons butter or margarine in a frying pan and fry on both sides until golden brown. Add more butter or margarine to the frying pan as necessary.

Serve with Russian dressing on the side.

YIELD:   *16 to 18 blintzes.*

*Advice from Mama:*   These blintzes make a nice meal with a green salad.

# Russian Dressing

*1 cup mayonnaise*
*½ cup ketchup*
*1 teaspoon garlic powder*

Mix mayonnaise, ketchup, and garlic powder together. Serve on salads, sandwiches, and blintzes with Reuben filling (page 106).

YIELD:    *1½ cups dressing.*

*Advice from Mama:*    If you have any dressing left over, cover well and refrigerate. It will last for months and can be used as a salad dressing or on sandwiches.

# Blintzes with Apple Filling

*2 cups apples, peeled, cored, and*
  *finely chopped*
*1 egg white*
*¼ cup chopped walnuts*
*1 tablespoon sugar*
*1 tablespoon lemon juice*

*¼ teaspoon ground cinnamon*
*16 to 18 prepared crepes for*
  *blintzes (page 98)*
*2 to 4 tablespoons butter or*
  *margarine for frying*

Mix first six ingredients together and place about 1 tablespoon filling in the center of a crepe. Fold the bottom of the crepe up over the filling. Fold opposite sides of the crepe in to meet in the middle. Now fold crepe over again to completely enclose the filling. Arrange filled crepes, fold side down, on a platter to wait until all the blintzes are made. (When blintzes are filled they can be frozen or refrigerated until ready to use.)

Melt 2 tablespoons butter or margarine in a frying pan and fry on both sides until golden brown. Add more butter or margarine to the frying pan as necessary. Serve hot.

YIELD:    *16 to 18 blintzes.*

# Blintzes with Apple Pie Filling

| | |
|---|---|
| *1 16-ounce can apple pie filling* | *1/2 teaspoon cinnamon* |
| *1 McIntosh apple, peeled, cored, and cut into small pieces* | *16 to 18 prepared crepes for blintzes (page 98)* |
| *Juice of 1/2 lemon* | *2 to 4 tablespoons butter or margarine for frying* |
| *1/4 cup chopped walnuts* | |

In a bowl mix apple pie filling, the fresh apple, lemon juice, walnuts, and cinnamon together. Place about 1 tablespoon filling in the center of a crepe. Fold the bottom of the crepe up over the filling. Fold opposite sides of the crepe in to meet in the middle. Now fold crepe over again to completely enclose the filling. Arrange filled crepes, fold side down, on a platter to wait until all the blintzes are made. (When blintzes are filled they can be frozen or refrigerated until ready to use.)

Melt 2 tablespoons butter or margarine in a frying pan and fry on both sides until golden brown. Add more butter or margarine to the frying pan as necessary. Serve hot.

Y I E L D :   *16 to 18 blintzes.*

# My Mother's Mock Blintzes

My mother concocted this dish when she'd rush home from work on a hot summer day and needed to make a quick dairy meal. So we were given a bowl of cold borscht, the mock blintzes, and a glass of milk. The real reason was that she didn't have enough money to buy steak or chops and this became a very economical meal. We loved these blintzes then, and I still do now.

| | |
|---|---|
| *1 pint dry cottage cheese or 1 pound farmer cheese* | *1 egg* |
| | *1/2 teaspoon salt* |

1 tablespoon sugar
4 eggs
¼ cup milk

8 Uneeda Biscuits
3 tablespoons butter or
    margarine for frying

Mix the cheese, 1 egg, salt, and sugar together and set aside. Beat the other 4 eggs and milk together in a bowl. Spread about 2 to 3 tablespoons of cheese mixture between 2 biscuits, making a sandwich. Melt the butter or margarine in a frying pan. Soak each biscuit sandwich in egg mixture until well softened. Place biscuit sandwiches in hot butter or margarine and sauté until brown on each side. Serve with jam, jelly, or sour cream.

YIELD:  *4 mock blintzes, enough for 2 normal eaters or 4 dieting eaters.*

# Knishes

Jews love a pastry with a filling, whether it's a sweet pastry pocket of hamantaschen, or a savory knish stuffed with mashed potatoes. On New York's Lower East Side there are still a handful of bakeries that make nothing but knishes. If you're not lucky enough to be able to get to one of these, you can still make your own. By the way, in case you don't know, in a knish you pronounce the *k* and the *n*. These knishes aren't at all the way my mother made them, but they're really much more like the traditional knishes. They take a little work, but you'll love the results. If you have an electric mixer, by all means use it to make the dough.

2 cups all-purpose flour
1 teaspoon baking powder
½ teaspoon salt
2 eggs, lightly beaten
3 tablespoons corn oil
3 tablespoons water
Potato filling (same as potato
    blintzes) (page 104)

or

Kasha filling (same as for kasha
    blintzes) (page 102)
Additional corn oil for brushing
    knishes

Sift the flour, baking powder, and salt into a mixing bowl or the bowl of an electric mixer. Make a well in the center and add the eggs, 1 tablespoon of oil, and 1 tablespoon of water. Use your hands or the dough hook of an electric mixer to blend ingredients together. Knead for 2 or 3 minutes, adding more oil and water (1 tablespoon at a time) to make a smooth dough. Continue kneading with an electric mixer, or remove to a lightly floured surface and knead 5 or 6 minutes by hand until dough becomes very smooth and elastic. Roll the dough into a ball and place it in an oiled bowl, cover, and let rest for 1 hour.

Preheat oven to 350°F. Lightly grease a baking sheet with vegetable oil.

Roll out the dough on a lightly floured board until very thin, approximately ⅛ inch thick. To get the dough as thin as possible, you will need to pull and stretch it as you roll it out, being careful all the while not to tear it. You should end up with a rectangle of rolled-out dough approximately 12 inches long (measured horizontally) and about 6 to 8 inches high (measured vertically).

Spread either potato filling or kasha filling smoothly over the entire surface of the dough, leaving a 1-inch margin all around. Gather up the dough at the bottom and roll up the dough like a jelly roll, placing it fold side down. Cut the roll into 3- to 4-inch sections, pinch the dough on the open ends closed, and place on prepared baking sheet. Brush the tops of the knishes with oil and bake at 350°F for approximately 45 minutes, until the knishes are golden brown.

YIELD:  *6 knishes.*

*Advice from Mama:*  Another way to make knishes is to roll out the dough as thin as possible, cut it into 3-inch circles or squares, place a tablespoon of filling on each circle or square of dough, and draw the edges together to make either a half-moon shape or a triangle. Pinch the edges together and bake as above.

# Potato Chremslach

Even if you never heard of "chremslach" before, I guarantee that you will love these golden, crispy balls of fried mashed potatoes.

| | |
|---|---|
| *6 medium potatoes* | *2 teaspoons salt* |
| *1 medium onion, diced* | *¼ teaspoon freshly ground* |
| *2 tablespoons corn oil* | *black pepper* |
| *4 eggs, lightly beaten* | *Corn oil for frying* |

Peel and slice the potatoes and boil them in salted water to cover until fully cooked. Drain and mash.

Sauté the onion in the corn oil until golden brown. Mix the onion into the mashed potatoes. Let mashed-potato mixture cool, then stir in eggs, salt, and pepper. Taste for seasoning and adjust as necessary.

Heat about 2 tablespoons of oil in a heavy frying pan. Drop mashed-potato mixture a tablespoonful at a time into the hot oil. Fry until golden brown on each side and remove to paper towel to drain. Repeat with remaining potato mixture, adding more oil to the frying pan as needed.

Serve while still warm with any meat or chicken dish. Potato chremslach are particularly good with sautéed calf's liver.

YIELD:    *6 to 8 servings.*

*Advice from Mama:*    Feel free to use leftover mashed potatoes in this recipe.

# Potato Latkes

The word "latke" means "pancake," but has come to mean more specifically the potato pancakes that are traditionally served during Chanukah. Although the potato was introduced rather late into

Jewish cooking, some time in the sixteenth century, when it was brought back to Europe from the Americas, the tradition of eating foods fried in oil during Chanukah goes back to ancient days and originates with the story told in the Talmud of the miracle that followed the destruction of the Second Temple by the Syrians. In the rubble of the Temple was found a single flask of oil, enough to keep the holy flame alive for just a single day. But to the astonishment of all, it burned for eight days! And from that time candles have been lit for the eight days of Chanukah, and foods like latkes fried in oil are eaten to celebrate the Feast of Lights.

My mother always grated her potatoes by hand and always, always she would scrape a little skin off her knuckle, making her hand bleed. To my cries of alarm she inevitably answered, "It's all right, *kinderle!* A little piece from my hand just makes the latkes taste better."

*4 large russet or Idaho potatoes*
*(about 1 pound each)*
*Juice of ½ lemon*
*1 large onion*
*2 large eggs*

*½ cup matzo meal or ¼ cup*
*flour*
*2 teaspoons salt*
*⅛ teaspoon white pepper*
*Corn oil for frying*

Peel the potatoes and grate them either by hand or in a food processor. Squeeze the grated potatoes by handfuls to get rid of excess starchy water. Another way to do this is to roll the grated potatoes in a clean kitchen towel and wring it out. Place the potatoes in a bowl and mix in the lemon juice. Peel and grate the onion and beat the eggs lightly. Add the grated onion, beaten eggs, matzo meal or flour, salt, and pepper, and mix well. Heat about ¼ cup of oil in a frying pan. Drop potato mixture into hot frying pan a tablespoon at a time and fry until brown on both sides. Drain on paper towels and keep latkes warm in a 250°F oven. Continue until all are done.

Serve immediately with either applesauce or sour cream.

YIELD:  *16 to 24 latkes, depending on the size of your tablespoon.*

*Advice from Mama:*  I was appearing on a radio talk show one day not that long ago and a lady called in to tell me how she fixes latkes ahead of time. Grate the potatoes, she said, mix with everything except the eggs. Break the eggs, beat them, and pour them over the latkes mixture. This keeps the air away from the potatoes, keeping them fresh and not discolored. Keep in the refrigerator until you're ready to fry them. Stir everything up and fry away. Sounds good.

# Soup Greens Latkes

I always thought this recipe was unique to my mother until I heard a man talking with longing and such nostalgia about *his* mother's soup greens latkes.

This is a recipe that illustrates perfectly the economy practiced in the Old World Jewish kitchen—a chicken is cooked with vegetables and water to make a soup. The broth is strained for clear soup—the first course. The vegetables are chopped up and turned into crisp latkes, which are served as a side dish with the boiled chicken from the soup. A delicious, homey meal that's great anytime, but particularly good when you're cold, you're tired, and you've been worrying too much.

*The cooked greens and root vegetables from chicken soup: parsley, dill, carrots, celery, onion, leek, and parsnip or any combination of the above*

*4 eggs, lightly beaten*
*1/2 cup matzo meal*
*1 teaspoon salt*
*1/8 teaspoon black pepper*
*Corn oil for frying*

Coarsely chop the greens and root vegetables. Mix together with eggs, matzo meal, salt, and pepper. Cover and let stand for 30 minutes. Heat 1/4 cup of oil in a heavy frying pan and drop batter a tablespoonful at a time into hot oil. Cook until brown on both sides.

Serve with the boiled chicken from the soup.

YIELD: *6 to 10 latkes, depending on the amount of soup greens from your soup. But you should get at least 6 latkes.*

# Cheese Latkes

Latkes of all kinds are usually beloved by everyone. This type, made with flour, wasn't served too often in my home. Usually the matzo meal latkes were made more often. But I think these are fluffier and lighter and have a completely different taste. They make Sunday breakfast a real treat.

| | |
|---|---|
| 8 ounces small-curd cottage cheese | 1/2 teaspoon salt |
| 4 eggs | 2 cups all-purpose flour |
| 2 tablespoons sugar | 1/2 teaspoon baking powder |
| | Butter or margarine for frying |

Place the cottage cheese in a fine-mesh strainer and let drain for several hours or overnight.

In a medium bowl beat together the eggs, sugar, and salt. Blend in flour and baking powder. Stir in cottage cheese and beat well. Cover and place mixture in the refrigerator for 30 minutes.

Heat 2 to 3 tablespoons butter or margarine in frying pan and drop tablespoonfuls of batter into the hot fat. Brown on both sides and remove to a warmed platter. Continue until all are done.

Serve with any topping you love: maple syrup, jam, sugar and cinnamon. . . .

YIELD: *12 to 14 latkes.*

# Fruit-Filled Chremslach

"Chremslach" or, about one hundred years ago, "grimslech," and sometimes "grimsel," are an ancient Jewish confection dating back to Roman days. The chremsel (singular of chremslach) was originally a fritter, fried in oil and drenched in honey. I don't remember my mother ever making this dish, but my friend Sylvia told me that her mother made prune-filled chremslach (without the sugar) and added them to pot roast! You live and learn.

*4 matzos*
*Boiling water*
*4 eggs, lightly beaten*
*½ cup matzo meal*

*¼ cup sugar*
*½ teaspoon salt*
*Butter or margarine for frying*

### Fruit for Filling

*Whole strawberries, stems*
  *removed*
*or*

*blueberries*
*or*
*whole pitted prunes*

Break the matzos into small pieces and put them in a bowl. Pour boiling water over the matzos to just cover. Set aside for 10 or 15 minutes. When the water has cooled and the matzos are soft, pour off the water and squeeze the matzos with your hands to remove excess moisture. Place the matzos in a bowl and stir in the eggs, matzo meal, sugar, and salt.

Cover and refrigerate for several hours or overnight to thicken.

Place a tablespoonful of matzo mixture in the palm of your hand and flatten to a disk about 2½ inches in diameter. Place either a whole strawberry or a teaspoon of blueberries or a whole pitted prune in the center. Fold edges of matzo dough around fruit. Dip your hands in cold water and shape the chremsel into a round or oval. When all are filled and shaped, fry them in hot butter or margarine until brown on both sides.

Serve with sour cream or yogurt.

YIELD: *12 to 16 chremslach.*

# Varenikis

"Vareniki"—the word is already plural—has been Americanized to "varenikis," probably on the theory that there can never be too many of these delicious dumplings on anyone's plate. They are claimed as a national dish by Ukrainians in particular, but are beloved by almost every other European nationality as well. There are variations, to be sure. Take cheese-filled varenikis, for example. I have seen grown men argue for hours about whether the filling should be sweet or savory. Litvaks—that is to say, Jews from Lithuania, mostly Vilna—consider themselves culturally and intellectually superior to other Jews and, looking down their noses as they do, wouldn't dream of eating the sweetened varenikis so popular with Polish or Galitzianer Jews. So, you see, a little salt or a little sugar can make one big deal of a difference.

My mother didn't make varenikis very often, mostly only in the summer when she could get fresh blueberries, and we just adored them. They were great hot, fresh out of the pot, with sour cream. If there were any leftovers, which was very rare, considering we were the three little pigs, my sisters and I, then Mama would sauté them in butter. That, of course, was absolutely delicious, too. As we ate, my mother would tell us a funny story about my father, who adored cheese varenikis. These were my grandmother's specialty, and he never seemed to get enough of them. One day she said, "All right, Chaim, I'm going to make so many varenikis, you wouldn't be able to finish them." She made him, my mother says, a huge pot full of varenikis! She spent all day cooking these for him. He took one look at that pot and he went crazy. He sat down and he devoured every single one of them. But the result was that a few hours later he was so sick that he never wanted to look at another cheese vareniki again. The moral was obvious. No matter how much you love something, don't be a pig and don't be greedy.

Varenikis were most commonly eaten as a dairy meal. A dairy meal consisted of a piece of fruit or melon before, or maybe a piece of herring, and then you'd have the varenikis, and then you'd have dessert and coffee. It was good then and it wouldn't be bad today.

## Dough

*2 cups all-purpose flour*          *½ cup milk*
*1 egg*                             *1 teaspoon salt*

Mix together the flour, egg, milk, and salt to make a workable dough. Add a few tablespoons of water if necessary. Remove to a lightly floured surface and knead for 10 to 15 minutes, until the dough feels smooth and satiny. Cover and let rest for 30 minutes.

Divide the dough in half. Cover one half to keep it from drying out. Roll out the other half on a well-floured surface until it is about ⅛ inch thick. Use a 2½- to 3-inch cookie cutter (if you're old-fashioned, use a *yohrzeit* glass) to cut out as many circles as possible. If the dough circles are well floured, you can stack them on a plate to wait until you have cut out all the dough and are ready to fill them.

Place 1 tablespoon of filling in the center of a circle of dough, fold over to make a half-moon shape, and pinch edges securely together. Arrange the varenikis in a single layer on a lightly floured board or cookie sheet. Now you can either freeze them to have for a future meal or cook them and eat them now.

*To freeze:* Line a cookie sheet with waxed paper and arrange the varenikis in one layer on the waxed paper, cover with waxed paper and arrange a second layer on top. Put in the freezer. When varenikis have frozen, place them in a plastic freezer bag or an airtight container and seal tightly. Do not thaw before cooking. When varenikis float to the surface, cook another 5 minutes.

*Cooking the varenikis:* Bring a large pot of lightly salted water to a boil. Drop in varenikis, no more than 10 or 12 at a time and cook, at a slow boil, until varenikis float to the top. Cook about 1 minute longer, if fresh (5 minutes longer, if frozen), and remove with a slotted spoon and place in a warmed bowl with a little butter or margarine. Repeat until all are cooked. Toss and serve with sour cream or yogurt.

*Variation:*   For fried varenikis, cook as described above. Drain on paper towels, then fry in butter or margarine until golden brown.

YIELD:   *50 to 60 varenikis, or enough for 4 to 6 servings.*

## Fillings for Varenikis

### Blueberry Filling

This was my mother's favorite filling for varenikis and is mine today. I still make these at my restaurant once in a while, and the reactions of my customers, and of my daughter, Robin, are just like mine were as a child. "Oooh, Ma!" they moan with great appreciation. "Varenikis!"

*1 pint fresh blueberries*
*¾ cup sugar*
*1 tablespoon fresh lemon juice*

*Sour cream or yogurt, for topping*

Pick over the blueberries to remove any stems or leaves. Wash them and place in a bowl together with sugar and lemon juice and mix well. Let stand for 20 to 30 minutes before filling. Serve with sour cream or yogurt on the side.

### Potato Filling

*3 large russet or Idaho potatoes*
*1 large onion, diced*
*3 tablespoons corn oil*
*1 tablespoon salt or less, to taste*
*1 teaspoon freshly ground black pepper or to taste*

*1 large onion, diced fine and sautéed until brown, in ¼ cup corn oil, for topping.*

Peel the potatoes, slice thin, and boil them in salted water to cover until they are tender. While they are cooking, sauté the onion in corn oil until it is a dark golden brown. Drain the potatoes and place them in a bowl. Mash them together with the sautéed onions. Season with salt and freshly ground black pepper to taste. Toss cooked varenikis with sautéed onion before serving.

## Savory Cheese Filling

1 pint small-curd cottage cheese
  or pot cheese
1 egg, beaten
3 tablespoons butter or
  margarine, softened to room
  temperature

1 teaspoon salt or to taste
1/4 teaspoon white pepper

Mash the cheese well with a fork. Beat in the egg, butter or margarine, salt, and pepper. Refrigerate filling for at least 1 hour before using.

## Sweet Cheese Filling

1 pint small-curd cottage cheese
  or pot cheese
1 egg, beaten
3 tablespoons butter or
  margarine, softened to room
  temperature

2 tablespoons sugar
1/8 teaspoon salt
Sour cream or yogurt, for
  topping

Mash the cheese well with a fork. Beat in the egg, butter, sugar, and salt. Refrigerate filling for at least 1 hour before using. Serve with sour cream or yogurt on the side.

## Cherry Filling

Sour cherries are traditional and the most delicious. These are hard to find except for a couple of weeks in the summer in some areas of the country. My mother only made these once a summer, because she had to pit the cherries, and of course that was a lot of work. Canned cherries are okay to use in this recipe. If the cherries are canned in water, simply drain them and proceed with the recipe; if they are canned in syrup, drain and reserve the syrup, and eliminate sugar from recipe below. Add the syrup to cherry juice and serve over the varenikis.

*2 cups pitted cherries*
*1/2 cup sugar*
*1 tablespoon lemon juice*
*1 tablespoon cornstarch*
*1 tablespoon cold water*

*1/4 cup melted butter, for topping*
*Sour cream or yogurt, for topping*

Place the cherries, sugar, and lemon juice in a saucepan. Mix the cornstarch with the cold water to make a smooth paste and add to the cherries. Cook over low heat for 10 to 15 minutes or until juice is no longer cloudy. Remove from heat and strain the cherries, reserving the juice. Serve the cherry juice, together with melted butter and sour cream, over cooked varenikis.

# 6

# FISH

□ □ □ □ □ □ □ □ □ □ □

To Jews living in Old World shtetls, freshwater fish was a luxury food, and often fillers were used in order to stretch the small amount of fresh fish that was affordable. The skin was saved intact and was wrapped around the fish mix in an attempt to make it look like a whole fish. Hence the derivation and invention of "gefilte fish," which was almost always served at the special Friday-night Sabbath meal. If a greater amount of fish was acquired, then it was pickled or salted in order to preserve it for days or even months. Most of the fish that was eaten in those days was salted and cured in some way, and that is why Jews are known for eating so much herring.

My mother's wonderful salmon croquettes are based on the principle of making a little go a long way, and we loved her dinner of croquettes, baked potatoes, and vegetables.

# Baked Fish with Garden Vegetables

My mother used to make this dish with just onions, string beans, and carrots. And she always used whitefish (the same fish she used to make gefilte fish), cleaned and cut into large chunks. Whitefish is a delicious fish for baking, but it has a lot of small bones and it tends to disintegrate when filleted and cooked. That's why I recommend the other choices. However, if you don't mind picking out the bones while you are eating, then go ahead and enjoy this delicious fish.

*2 or 3 stalks broccoli, cut into flowerets and bite-size chunks*

*1 head cauliflower, cut into flowerets and bite-size chunks*

*3 carrots, cut in half and sliced into 2-inch sticks*

*1/2 pound string beans, stem ends removed, and snapped in half*

*1 small zucchini, cut into bite-size pieces*

*1 yellow summer squash, cut into bite-size pieces*

*1 red bell pepper, seeded and cut into bite-size pieces*

*1 green bell pepper, seeded and cut into bite-size pieces*

*4 ripe tomatoes, cut into bite-size pieces*

*1 onion, sliced*

*1 clove garlic, crushed*

*3 to 4 tablespoons butter, margarine, or oil*

*2 packages MBT instant chicken broth*

*Butter or oil for baking pan*

*4 to 8 pieces of filleted firm fish such as salmon, cod, scrod, etc.*

In a large skillet or sauté pan sauté all the vegetables and garlic in butter, margarine, or oil, tossing with a spatula to mix everything together. Sauté for 5 minutes, sprinkle with MBT instant chicken broth, mix well, and remove from heat.

Preheat oven to 375°F. Butter or oil the bottom and sides of a baking pan large enough to hold the fish and vegetables.

Place the fish fillets in the baking pan, cover with the sautéed vegetables, and cover the pan tightly with tinfoil. Bake in pre-heated oven for 20 minutes. Serve with kasha or any rice dish.

YIELD:   *4 to 8 servings.*

# Poached Salmon

Poached salmon wasn't anything my mother had in her shtetl! And it's very expensive today as well. But it makes a beautiful and special buffet dish that is also extremely easy to prepare. It's good hot or cold and will feed a lot of people.

*6- to 9-pound salmon*
*1 stalk celery, cut into large*
  *chunks*
*1 small onion, quartered*
*2 sprigs parsley*

*1 tablespoon kosher salt*
*½ teaspoon white pepper*
*Fresh dill sprigs*
*2 lemons, thinly sliced*

Ask the fish market to fillet the whole salmon, leaving on the skin and saving the head and bones for you. Wash the salmon fillets and set aside.

Place the bones and head in a shallow roasting pan or fish poacher. Add the celery, onion, parsley, salt, and pepper. Add enough cold water to just cover all the ingredients by 1 inch. Simmer gently for 20 minutes. Add the salmon fillets, cover, and poach at the lowest simmer for 15 minutes. Remove from heat, uncover, and let the fillets cool in the poaching liquid. Carefully remove the fish fillets using two large spatulas, or even scooping it up with both your hands. Place, skin side down, on a large platter lined with lettuce. If you prefer, you can gently pull away the skin first. Poke a sprig of fresh dill through the center of each lemon slice and decorate the fish with lemon slices. Serve the salmon at room temperature or chilled with Cucumber-Dill Sauce (page 124).

Strain the liquid and freeze to use as fish stock. Pick away any meat left on the bones and mix with a little mayonnaise to make a salad.

YIELD:  *10 to 12 servings.*

*Advice from Mama:*

1. If you prefer, you can poach a salmon whole, if you have a fish poacher or a deep enough roasting pan. The water must come level with the fish. Ask your fishmonger to remove the eyes, gut, and clean the whole salmon. Simmer water and vegetables for 20 minutes. Measure the fish with a ruler at the thickest point. Allow 10 minutes cooking time for each inch of thickness. Let the salmon cool in the poaching liquid. Remove from liquid to a platter. Carefully peel away the skin, but leave the head on. Decorate with lemon slices as above.
2. If you're preparing this for a family meal and you don't want to be fancy, you can have the salmon cut into steaks. Make the poaching liquid with the vegetables and water as for the poached fillets. Measure the thickness of the steaks and allow 10 minutes cooking time for every inch.

# Cucumber-Dill Sauce

*2 cucumbers, peeled and seeded and roughly chopped*
*6 sprigs fresh dill*
*1 cup sour cream*

*½ cup mayonnaise*
*1 teaspoon prepared horseradish (white)*

Place all the ingredients in a blender or food processor and blend for 1 minute. Pass in a serving bowl as an accompaniment to Poached Salmon (page 123).

YIELD:  *Approximately 2 cups.*

# Fried Smelts

❧

There were only four ways and three types of fish that were prepared and served to us when I was growing up—there was gefilte
fish, baked whitefish, fried flounder, and fried smelts. The smelts
were my favorite. If they were very tiny, we would eat them bones
and all. If they were large smelts, we would slit the fish along the
back, lift the flesh and remove the spine. Either way, they are
really good, with a sweet flavor.

| | |
|---|---|
| *20 to 24 smelts, heads removed* | *2 teaspoons salt* |
| *3 eggs* | *¼ teaspoon white pepper* |
| *¼ cup water* | *½ cup corn or safflower oil* |
| *½ cup flour* | *2 medium onions, sliced* |
| *1 cup matzo meal* | |

Wash smelts and pat dry with paper towel. Mix eggs and water
together. In a separate bowl mix together flour, matzo meal, salt,
and pepper. Dip smelts in beaten eggs and dredge in flour-matzo
mixture. Heat the oil and sauté the onions for a few minutes. Push
the onions to the side and fry the smelts for a few minutes on each
side. Continue cooking the onions on the side of the pan until all
the smelts are fried. The fried smelts should be golden and crisp
and the onions should be a dark golden brown. Serve with boiled,
parsleyed potatoes and a green vegetable.

YIELD:  *4 to 6 servings.*

# Fried Herring

❧

Fried herring is delicious for breakfast or brunch with scrambled
eggs. If you have Romanian roots, you'll probably love it the way
my friend Philip Turner does—served with Mamaliga (page 93)
and cottage cheese for Sunday-night supper.

1 cup all-purpose flour
1/2 teaspoon salt
1/2 teaspoon pepper
3 eggs

1/4 cup water
1/2 cup butter or corn oil
4 matjes herring fillets

Season the flour with salt and pepper. Beat eggs together with the water. Heat the butter or oil in a heavy frying pan. Dredge herring fillets in flour, dip in eggs, and dredge in flour again. Fry the herring fillets over moderate heat so that they cook slowly, turning them over several times while they cook. When they are done they should be crisp and a nice golden brown color.

YIELD:   4 to 8 servings (some people eat half a fillet, some people like a whole one).

# Salmon Croquettes

Whenever my mother didn't have enough money (which was often) or she planned on a meal that didn't require using the oven on a hot summer day, she'd buy a couple of cans of salmon and make these delicious croquettes. Of course, in those days canned salmon was relatively inexpensive.

1 pound fresh salmon fillet
or
1 15 1/2-ounce can salmon (red or pink)
1 medium onion, diced
2 tablespoons butter or margarine

2 eggs
Salt to taste
1/4 teaspoon white pepper
1/2 cup matzo meal
1/4 cup corn oil
1 egg, beaten
Additional matzo meal

Poach the salmon fillet for 10 minutes in 1 cup simmering, salted water. Remove from heat and let cool in the liquid. Sauté the onion in butter or margarine until translucent but not brown. Remove skin from the salmon and reserve cooking liquid. If you are using canned salmon, drain the salmon but reserve the liquid. Crumble the salmon into a bowl, removing skin and bones, and add ¼ cup liquid. Add the sautéed onions, eggs, salt, pepper, and matzo meal. Mix well to make a mixture that just holds together. If too dry, add more liquid; if too wet, add a little more matzo meal. Taste to see if salt is needed. Shape the mixture into 4 or 6 oval croquettes.

Heat the oil in a skillet. Dip each croquette in beaten egg and coat with matzo meal. Sauté in hot oil until brown on each side. Serve hot with Lemon-Parsley Sauce (page 127) or plain with lemon wedges.

YIELD:   *4 to 6 croquettes.*

*Advice from Mama:*   These croquettes may be frozen before or after cooking. Also they reheat very well. Simply pop them in a preheated 350°F oven for about 15 minutes.

# Lemon-Parsley Sauce

| | |
|---|---|
| *¼ cup butter or margarine* | *or* |
| *¼ cup flour* | *2 cups chicken broth* |
| *1 Knorr chicken bouillon cube,* | *Juice of 2 lemons* |
| *dissolved in 2 cups hot water* | *2 tablespoons chopped parsley* |

In a small, heavy saucepan heat the butter or margarine and stir in flour to make a roux. Cook, stirring, over medium heat for 2 to 3 minutes. Gradually stir in the bouillon or broth and cook, stirring, over moderate heat until thickened (5 to 10 minutes). Stir in the juice of 2 lemons, then add the lemon halves from which the juice has been squeezed. Simmer for 5 minutes, remove from heat, remove the lemon halves and discard. Stir in chopped parsley. If the sauce seems too thick to you, stir in a little hot water.

This sauce looks and tastes great and is an excellent accompaniment for Salmon Croquettes (page 126) or any plain broiled fish.

YIELD: *About 2 cups of sauce.*

# 7

# POLTRY

□ □ □ □ □ □ □ □ □ □ □ □ □ □ □ □ □ □ □ □ □ □ □

I n the old country Jews didn't keep pets, they kept chickens. Every household had a few chickens scratching around in the yard. To have chickens meant, first of all, that you had a good supply of eggs, and every once in a while, when a hen got too old to produce eggs anymore, she went into the pot. Eating a chicken was no casual thing and it was either a major holiday or the result of some great necessity. There's even an old saying that goes, "When a Jewish farmer eats a chicken, one of them is sick."

I used to love to go to the kosher butcher with my mother when I was growing up. It looked like any other butcher shop except for the types of meat that were carried, and the man behind the counter always handed me a delicious slice of boiled salami. At the kosher butcher one would never buy a chicken that was already dead. A live chicken was selected, approved by my mother, then killed. The dead chicken was turned over to a woman who was called the "chicken plucker," who proceeded to pluck the feathers from the chicken so rapidly that the whole process took only a few minutes. My mother always felt sorry for this poor woman, who was doing what my mother considered the most menial of jobs. The women who took these jobs were either widowed or so poor that they had to help support their families (in those days it was not usual for a woman to work outside the home). Being a chicken plucker was one of the few jobs available to these women.

Today, chicken is one of the most versatile foods available and one I never get tired of preparing. When I was growing up, chicken was always served for the Friday Sabbath meal, and it was always boiled. That way my mother could get two courses out of one chicken—chicken soup and boiled chicken. Roasting a chicken seemed very wasteful and extravagant, because what you ended up with was just one thing—roast chicken. Delicious, but not for the likes of us. When we had complained incessantly, begging her to make a roast chicken for a change, Mama tried to appease us by taking the boiled chicken, seasoning it with salt and pepper, and roasting it in the oven to brown the skin. "Forget it!" we told her. This second version was even worse than the original plain boiled chicken. Gradually Mama started to add chicken to the midweek menu, and that's when her marvelous cooking abilities shone.

## Plain Roast Chicken

Why should I write a recipe for plain roast chicken? Well, you'd be surprised how many times that's really all that people want. After making all the different foods that I do, often my kids say, "Ma! How about some plain roast chicken?" And when I make it—and it's so easy—we all dig in and enjoy.

3½- to 4-pound roasting chicken  |  1 teaspoon paprika
or  |  ¼ teaspoon black pepper
4- to 6-pound oven stuffer  |  ½ teaspoon poultry seasoning
   roaster  |     (optional)
1 tablespoon garlic powder  |  2 tablespoons corn oil
1 teaspoon salt

Preheat oven to 375°F.

Wash chicken thoroughly, removing any excess fat or pinfeathers. Dry well with paper towels. Mix together the garlic powder, salt, paprika, pepper, and poultry seasoning if desired. Rub the chicken with corn oil, then rub the spices all over the bird. Tuck the wings under and place in roasting pan. Roast in preheated oven, 1 hour to 1 hour and 15 minutes for the smaller bird, 1½ to 2 hours for the larger oven stuffer roaster. Baste chicken two or three times while roasting. If the chicken is stuffed, add 30 minutes to the roasting time (see Bread Stuffing, page 146). The chicken is done when juices run clear when thigh is pricked. Remove from oven and let stand 15 to 20 minutes before carving.

YIELD:  *2 to 8 servings, depending on size of bird.*

# Helzel

This was a delicacy my mother made whenever she bought a large chicken and had the time to spare for fussing with stuffing a tube of skin from the chicken's neck. "Helzel" means the neck skin of a chicken (duck, turkey, or goose would qualify as well). When she purchased her fresh-killed chicken she would admonish the butcher to be careful and not tear the neck when he severed the head and gullet. The head was discarded, the feathers collected and sold to the pillow man, and the rest of the chicken was cooked and eaten, even the feet. When the neck is cut away from the chicken, a tube of skin with an opening at each end remains. My mother would have me thread a large needle with heavy white cotton thread and she would sew one end of the neck closed. She would then stuff the neck and sew closed the other end. It was cooked in one of several ways. One was to cook it while making Chicken Soup (page 64), poaching it along with the other ingredients. The second way was to cook it along with the ingredients of her delicious Chicken and Meatball Fricassee (page 142). And sometimes she might roast it in the same pan along with the Plain Roast Chicken (page 130). Whichever way it was cooked, it was cut in slices before serving, and whoever got one of the ends had to pull out the white threads.

If you would like to try making helzel yourself, you will need to find a live poultry market so you can get the neck skin without it being slit up the side. You can use the neck of a large chicken, duck, goose, or turkey (a smaller neck will hardly be worth the trouble).

¼ cup Schmaltz (rendered
  chicken fat) (page 10)
1 small onion, finely chopped
½ cup matzo meal
¼ cup fine bread crumbs
1 egg, beaten

1 teaspoon salt
¼ teaspoon paprika
1 neck skin from a large
  chicken, duck, goose, or
  turkey

Heat the schmaltz in a skillet and sauté the onion in it until golden brown. Remove from heat and mix together with matzo meal, bread crumbs, egg, salt, and paprika. Sew up one end of whatever poultry skin you are using. Push stuffing gently inside the poultry neck. The stuffing will expand and stretch the neck as it cooks, so don't fill the neck to overflowing. Carefully sew the other end closed.

YIELD:   *1 stuffed poultry neck.*

# Roast Lemon-Garlic Chicken

One of my best recipes, this chicken is delectable. It is also a perfect dish for someone on a salt-free diet. It has so much flavor you'll never miss the salt. I developed this salt-free recipe because so many people would ask me if I served any salt-free dishes. Happily, this recipe became everyone's favorite and I think it will become one of yours, too.

*8 cloves garlic, crushed*　　　　　*Corn oil*
*Juice of 2 lemons*　　　　　　　*Garlic powder*
*3 tablespoons honey*　　　　　　*Paprika*
*2 chickens (3 to 3½ pounds*
　*each), split in half*

Preheat oven to 375°F.

Mix together crushed garlic, lemon juice, and honey and set aside.

Place the halved chickens, skin side up, in a shallow roasting pan. Brush the chickens with corn oil. Generously sprinkle garlic powder on chickens and then sprinkle with paprika. Bake in a preheated oven for 30 minutes.

Remove pan from oven and carefully pour garlic, lemon, honey mixture over the chicken. Put back in oven and bake for an additional 30 to 40 minutes, until chicken is very brown.

YIELD:　*4 to 6 servings.*

# Chicken Cutlets

꙳

Did your mother or *bubbie* ever make this dish? Well, mine didn't either. But who cares—it's delicious anyway.

*4 whole chicken breasts, split and boned with skin removed*
*3 eggs*
*2 teaspoons garlic powder*
*¹/₂ teaspoon white pepper*
*2 teaspoons salt*

*1 cup matzo meal*
*4 tablespoons corn oil, butter, or margarine*
*Mustard-Dill Sauce (below)*
*or*
*Garlic Sauce (page 135)*

Pound the chicken cutlets, shiny side up, between two pieces of waxed paper, to make them thinner. Beat the eggs together with 1 teaspoon garlic powder, ¹/₄ teaspoon white pepper, and 1 teaspoon salt. In another bowl combine matzo meal with 1 teaspoon garlic powder, ¹/₄ teaspoon pepper, and 1 teaspoon salt. Mix well.

Dip cutlets in egg mixture and then in matzo meal. Press matzo meal into the cutlets with your hands to make sure it sticks. Sauté cutlets in oil, butter, or margarine, 3 to 5 minutes on each side, until golden brown. Serve hot with either Mustard-Dill Sauce or with Garlic Sauce.

YIELD: *6 to 8 servings.*

# Mustard-Dill Sauce

꙳

*¹/₄ cup corn oil or margarine*
*¹/₄ cup all-purpose flour*
*2 cups chicken broth*

*2 tablespoons Dijon-style mustard*
*¹/₂ cup fresh dill, finely chopped*

In a saucepan heat the oil or margarine. Gradually stir in flour and cook, stirring for about 5 minutes to make a roux. Gradually stir in the chicken broth and cook, stirring until heated through and thickened, about 5 to 10 minutes. If the sauce seems too thick, add some more broth or water. Remove from heat and stir in mustard and dill.

Serve with Chicken Cutlets (page 134), Poached Salmon (page 123), or any plain broiled fish to add zip.

YIELD: *About 2½ cups.*

# Garlic Sauce

*¼ cup corn oil or margarine*       *2 cups chicken broth*
*¼ cup all-purpose flour*           *Salt to taste*
*2 cloves garlic, crushed*

In a saucepan heat the oil or margarine. Gradually stir in flour and cook, stirring, for about 5 minutes to make a roux. Stir in crushed garlic and cook, stirring 1 minute longer. Gradually stir in the chicken broth and cook, stirring until heated through and thickened, about 5 to 10 minutes. If the sauce seems too thick, add more broth or water. Remove from heat and taste for seasoning. Add salt if necessary. Serve with Chicken Cutlets (page 134).

YIELD: *About 2 cups.*

# Boneless Stuffed Chicken

---

*1 package frozen chopped
  spinach*
*1 cup bread crumbs*
*1 small onion, finely minced*
*½ pound small mushrooms,
  sliced*
*2 tablespoons corn oil*
*2 cloves garlic, put through a
  garlic press*

*2 teaspoons salt*
*¼ teaspoon black pepper*
*1 egg*
*6 whole chicken breasts, boned,
  skin left on*
*Corn oil*
*Garlic powder*
*Salt*

Cook the spinach according to package directions, drain and squeeze dry. In a large mixing bowl combine spinach with the bread crumbs and mix well. Sauté the onion and mushrooms in oil until softened. Add these to the spinach and bread crumbs, along with the garlic, salt, and pepper. When the mixture is completely cool, add the egg and mix well.

Preheat oven to 375°F.

Use your fingers to loosen the skin on the chicken, making pockets for the stuffing. Stuff the pockets with the spinach–bread crumb mix. Place the chicken breasts, skin side up, in a roasting pan. If there is any stuffing left over, place some underneath each chicken breast. Brush skin with oil and sprinkle with garlic powder and salt. Bake in a preheated oven for 45 minutes to 1 hour, until done.

YIELD:  *6 to 8 servings.*

# Stuffed Chicken Breasts with Mushroom Sauce

This makes a wonderful buffet dish, and I've served it at several weddings I've catered. It holds up nicely in a chafing dish and goes well with almost any side dish you like.

*4 large whole chicken breasts,
    boned, split, and skinned
1 stick butter or margarine
1 large onion, minced fine
2 cloves garlic, crushed
1 cup bread crumbs, unseasoned*

*1 tablespoon grated Gruyère or
    Parmesan cheese
1 teaspoon salt
1/4 teaspoon freshly ground
    black pepper*

### For the Mushroom Sauce

*1/4 cup flour
1/4 cup melted butter or
    margarine
1 cup chicken stock
1 cup dry white wine
or*

*2 cups chicken stock (and leave
    out wine)
12 mushrooms, sliced
Salt to taste
Watercress leaves or parsley for
    garnish*

Preheat oven to 375°F.

Flatten each chicken breast with a mallet or the flat side of a meat cleaver, pounding the breast on the shiny side.

Prepare the stuffing. Reserve 2 tablespoons of the butter or margarine. Melt the rest in a heavy skillet and sauté the onion and garlic until onion turns golden brown. Remove from heat and stir in the bread crumbs, cheese, salt, and pepper. Mix well. If mixture is very dry, add a tablespoon or two of chicken stock.

Lay the chicken breasts on a flat surface so the shiny sides are down. Place a tablespoonful of stuffing on each chicken breast and roll up like a jelly roll to enclose the stuffing. Place folded side down in a lightly oiled gratin or other ovenproof dish. Melt the reserved 2 tablespoons of butter or margarine and lightly brush each breast with it. Bake in preheated oven for 30 minutes.

In the meantime prepare the mushroom sauce. In a saucepan stir the flour into the ¼ cup melted margarine or butter and cook, stirring, over low heat for 1 minute. Add the chicken stock and wine, whisking it in a little at a time so that there are no lumps. If you can't avoid lumps, put into blender or strain through a sieve and replace in pan. Simmer, stirring frequently, until the sauce begins to thicken. Add the sliced mushrooms and cook for about 5 minutes. Taste for seasoning and add salt if necessary.

Arrange the chicken breasts on a serving platter, pour a little mushroom gravy over all the breasts, and serve the rest in a gravy boat. Garnish with watercress or parsley.

YIELD: *4 to 8 servings, depending.*

*Advice from Mama:* Eliminate the cheese if you are cooking kosher and increase the salt slightly.

# Chicken Salad

Chicken salad makes great sandwiches, but it also makes a lovely and delicious salad plate for lunch. Line a dinner plate with green leaf lettuce, place a serving of chicken salad in the center, and then surround with various fresh garden vegetables.

*1 large roasted chicken, cooled to room temperature (page 130)*
*or*
*1 large boiled chicken from Chicken Soup (page 64)*

*3 stalks celery, without leaves*
*2 scallions*
*1 pinch white pepper*
*6 or more tablespoons mayonnaise*

Cut as much meat as possible away from the bone. Remove all skin, fat, and cartilage. Cut boned chicken into bite-size chunks.

Dice celery and and slice scallions crosswise, including green part. Add pepper and mayonnaise and mix well. Yummy!

YIELD: *8 servings.*

# Chicken Pot Pie

### Chicken

*1 oven stuffer roaster chicken, weighing 5 to 6 pounds*
*4 quarts water*
*1 tablespoon kosher salt*
*1 teaspoon white pepper*

*3 stalks celery*
*1 large onion, quartered*
*1 carrot, peeled*
*¼ cup parsley, chopped*
*2 sprigs fresh dill (optional)*

### For Pie

*4 carrots*
*2 large potatoes*
*2 stalks celery*
*2 onions*
*¼ cup margarine or corn oil*
*½ cup flour*
*4 to 6 cups chicken broth*
*2 bay leaves*

*1 Knorr chicken bouillon cube*
*1 teaspoon garlic powder*
*¼ teaspoon white pepper*
*1 package frozen peas*
*1 unbaked frozen 2-crust pie shell, defrosted*
*1 egg, lightly beaten*

Prepare the chicken for the pie. Place the chicken in a large pot together with the water, salt, pepper, celery, onion, parsley, and dill. Bring to a boil, lower to a simmer, and skim away any scum that has risen to the surface. Let simmer for 1 to 1½ hours, until the chicken is tender. Remove from heat and take the chicken out of the broth and allow to cool. Strain the broth and save the vegetables for Soup Greens Latkes (page 113). Reserve the broth. Remove skin from the chicken and discard. Pull away meat from the bones and cut up any large pieces into bite-size pieces. Refrigerate until needed.

Prepare the vegetables. Peel the carrots and potatoes and cut into bite-size pieces. Cut the celery stalks into bite-size pieces. Peel and roughly chop the onions. Place the carrots and potatoes in a pot with 4 cups water. Bring to a boil and cook for 10 minutes. Add celery and onions and cook until potatoes are tender. Drain and reserve the vegetables.

Heat the margarine or corn oil in a heavy pot and stir in the flour. Cook, stirring, over medium heat for 3 to 4 minutes. Gradually stir in 4 cups chicken stock and simmer, stirring frequently until slightly thickened. Add the bay leaves, bouillon cube, garlic powder, and white pepper. Simmer for 15 minutes. If sauce is too thick, add chicken broth to thin it out. Remove from heat and discard the bay leaves. Add reserved vegetables, frozen peas, and cut-up chicken pieces.

Preheat oven to 375°F.

Divide the chicken and vegetables between two ovenproof casseroles or soufflé dishes. Cover the top with the defrosted pie pastry. Poke a few holes in the pastry with a fork. Brush with the beaten egg and bake in preheated oven for 30 minutes or until pie pastry is golden brown.

Serve with crusty bread and a salad.

Y I E L D :   *2 chicken pot pies, each serving 4 people.*

# Spicy Chicken Stew

I learned this recipe from my Jamaican cook, Eunel, who made it one day for the restaurant staff. We loved it so much I added it to the menu. A little Jewish, a little Jamaican, and very delicious.

*2 chickens, each weighing about
    3 1/2 pounds
1/2 cup corn oil
8 cloves garlic, crushed
2 medium onions, diced large*

*6 ripe tomatoes, peeled, seeded,
    and roughly chopped
4 green bell peppers, cored,
    seeded, and roughly chopped
1 tablespoon kosher salt*

*½ tablespoon freshly ground          3 cups water*
  *black pepper*

Have the butcher cut each chicken into ten pieces. Wash and dry the chicken pieces. Heat the corn oil in a heavy skillet and brown the chicken pieces together with half the garlic in the hot oil. As they are browned, place each piece of chicken in a large ovenproof casserole or roasting pan. Discard the oil when all the chicken is browned.

Preheat oven to 375°F.

Add the remaining garlic, onions, tomatoes, bell peppers, salt, pepper, and water to the chicken and mix well. Cover and cook in preheated oven for 1 hour.

Serve over rice or noodles.

YIELD: *6 to 8 servings.*

*Advice from Mama:*   You can also use parts of chicken already cut up in the supermarket. For example, you can use all drumsticks, or all thighs. So shop around and get whatever is on sale that day.

# Chicken and Meatball Fricassee

This recipe was always a family favorite and is now the most popular dish I serve in my restaurant and take-out store. The combination of flavors is delicious and makes for a very comforting, *haimish* (cozy or homey), and satisfying dish. Best of all, it reheats and reheats and reheats.

*1 pound ground chuck*
*1 small onion, diced fine*
*2 cloves garlic, crushed, or 1 teaspoon garlic powder (if you're in a rush!)*
*1 1/2 to 2 teaspoons salt*
*1/4 teaspoon pepper*
*1 egg*
*1/4 cup water*
*1/3 cup matzo meal*
*2 small chickens (2 1/2 to 3 pounds each), each cut into 8 pieces*

*Giblets from the chickens, including livers, if you wish\**
*4 carrots, peeled and diced*
*2 medium onions, peeled and diced*
*4 cloves garlic, crushed*
*2 teaspoons kosher salt*
*3 bay leaves*
*1 cup ketchup*
*3 cups water, or enough to cover chicken pieces halfway*

Preheat oven to 375°F.

In a bowl mix together the ground chuck, onion, garlic, salt, pepper, egg, and water. Knead together with your hands until well mixed, then blend in matzo meal. Use your hands to form small meatballs about the size of a walnut. Arrange them on an ungreased baking sheet or in a roasting pan and bake in the preheated oven for 15 to 20 minutes, until they firm up. Remove meatballs but do not turn off the oven.

While the meatballs are in the oven, wash the chicken pieces and remove any excess fat. If you're very fussy, you can also remove

---

\* My mother reserved the livers as a delicacy for other dishes. But other people's mothers made fricassee that included the livers. This is also very delicious, so I leave it up to you as to whether to include the livers or not. That is, of course, if the cat doesn't get them first.

the skin. Wash the giblets and the livers. Arrange the chicken, giblets, livers, meatballs, carrots, onions, and garlic in a large Dutch oven or heavy casserole with a tight-fitting lid. Add the salt and bay leaves. Dissolve the ketchup in 3 cups of water and pour over all the ingredients. The liquid should come halfway up the solid ingredients. Add more water if necessary. Cover and bake for 1½ to 2 hours. Skim away any visible fat and serve immediately, or cool and refrigerate overnight. Remove all pieces of congealed fat. Reheat and serve. This fricassee can be reheated day after day. It just gets better.

YIELD: *6 to 8 servings.*

# Lima Bean–Chicken Casserole

This is definitely a "Leah" recipe and not something I ever got at home. I concocted it because I love lima beans, I love chicken, and I love making casseroles because they are the perfect one-dish meal. It turned out to be perfectly scrumptious, so I make it often for family and for company.

*1 cup dried lima beans*
*8 cups water*
*1 teaspoon salt*
*2 tablespoons corn oil*
*1 onion, finely chopped*
*1 clove garlic, crushed*
*1 teaspoon salt*

*¼ teaspoon pepper*
*3½- to 4-pound chicken, cut up*
  *into 8 pieces*
*Garlic powder*
*Paprika*
*Salt*

Soak lima beans in water overnight. Drain, put in pot with 8 cups fresh water and 1 teaspoon salt. Bring to a boil, reduce to a gentle simmer and cook about 1 to 1½ hours, until beans are tender. Drain the beans and reserve ½ cup liquid.
Preheat oven to 375°F.

Heat the oil in a skillet and sauté the onion and garlic until golden brown. Spread the browned onion and garlic in the bottom of a baking dish. Add the lima beans, the reserved ½ cup liquid from cooking the lima beans, 1 teaspoon salt, and the pepper. Mix well. Place chicken pieces on top of lima beans, sprinkle with garlic powder, paprika, and salt. Bake, uncovered, in a preheated oven for 1 hour or until chicken is browned.

YIELD:  *4 to 6 servings.*

# Fricassee of Chicken Giblets

The only time my mother ever made this dish was when we were having company and she had to buy one or two extra chickens. This gave her extra wings and giblets. Sometimes she would add small meatballs (see Chicken and Meatball Fricassee, page 142) to stretch it even further. This is a wonderful dish, tasty with a capital *T* for taste. And it is even better when made a day ahead and reheated.

Incidentally, the chicken livers were always set aside, cooked and chopped with grieben and hard-boiled egg for a special appetizer treat.

*6 to 8 chicken wings*
*8 to 10 each of the chicken*
  *giblets*
*2 medium carrots, scraped and*
  *diced*
*1 medium onion, peeled and*
  *diced*

*4 cloves garlic, crushed*
*1 teaspoon salt*
*¼ cup ketchup*
*1 cup water*
*1 bay leaf*

Preheat oven to 375°F.
Place all the ingredients in a small Dutch oven with a tight-fitting lid. Cover and bake for 1½ hours. Remove from oven. Tilt the pot

to one side and skim off as much fat as possible, or refrigerate overnight and remove congealed cold fat. Reheat and serve. This is good as an appetizer or a main course served with rice.

YIELD:  *2 main course servings, 6 appetizer servings.*

*Advice from Mama:*

1. If you buy your chickens one at a time, you can save up wings and giblets by wrapping them up and freezing them until you have enough to make this recipe.
2. This dish is even more wonderful if you add a stuffed Helzel (page 131) to the pot when cooking.

## Roast Turkey with Gravy

Turkey! It's without a doubt one of the most versatile foods available. It's low in cholesterol and fat in general. It's always festive and delicious and, best of all, easy to make. It goes a long way in feeding a crowd, and any leftovers can be used to make a soup, sandwich, or casserole.

| | |
|---|---|
| *1 turkey with giblets* | *2 teaspoons garlic powder* |
| *Bread Stuffing (page 146)* | *1 stalk celery* |
| *Garlic powder* | *1 teaspoon salt* |
| *Salt* | *½ cup flour* |
| *4 to 8 cups water* | *½ cup cold water* |
| *1 small onion* | *Kitchen Bouquet (optional)* |

Preheat oven to 375°F.

Stuff the turkey and sprinkle the outside generously with garlic powder and salt and rub into the skin. Place in a roasting pan and tuck in the wings. Do not tie the legs. Cover completely with tinfoil, making a tent. Try not to have the tinfoil press against the skin. Calculate the roasting time at 15 minutes for each pound for a small turkey; 10 minutes per pound if over 18 pounds. Roast the turkey in the preheated oven. One hour before time is up, remove the foil and baste with accumulated pan juices. Repeat in 30 minutes. Remove the turkey and let rest in pan to cool slightly.

While the turkey is roasting, place the giblets and 4 cups water (for a small turkey, 8 cups for a large turkey) in a saucepan. Add the onion, garlic powder, celery, and salt. Bring to a boil, skim away any scum that has risen to the surface and reduce heat to a simmer. Cook for about 1 hour, until the giblets are tender. Strain the stock and reserve.

Remove the turkey to a serving platter. Pour the giblet stock into the roasting pan and scrape the bottom with a wooden spoon to get all the drippings. Pour the stock and drippings back into saucepan. Place over medium heat. Dissolve the flour in ½ cup cold water and stir into simmering broth. Simmer until gravy has thickened. Taste and adjust the salt if necessary. Add a few drops of Kitchen Bouquet for color.

YIELD: *Depends on size of turkey.*

# Bread Stuffing

*2 small loaves white bread, sliced*
*1 large onion, finely diced*
*1 stalk celery, finely diced*
*1 clove garlic, crushed*
*2 tablespoons corn oil or margarine*

*1 teaspoon salt*
*½ teaspoon freshly ground black pepper*
*½ teaspoon poultry seasoning*
*½ cup chicken broth or as necessary*

Lay the bread slices on a rack in the oven for several hours or overnight to dry them out.

Sauté the onion, celery, and garlic in corn oil until translucent. Do not brown. Stir in salt, pepper, and poultry seasoning. Transfer the sautéed vegetables to a large mixing bowl and crumble the bread into the vegetables. Mix well. Gradually add the broth and continue mixing. If it seems too dry, add more broth, but not so much as to make it mushy. If the stuffing is for a chicken, leave it a little dry because the juices from the bird will moisten it.

YIELD:  *About 10 cups.*

*Advice from Mama:*

1. If there is stuffing left over, bake it for 1 hour in a well-greased ovenproof dish. Serve as a side dish.
2. You can substitute any other kind of bread you like, or even a mix of breads.
3. If you substitute thyme for the poultry seasoning, this stuffing is great for a Roast Stuffed Leg of Lamb (page 176).

# Roast Duck

| | |
|---|---|
| *1 duck (3 1/2 to 4 1/2 pounds)* | *Salt* |
| *1 orange, peeled* | *Garlic powder* |

Preheat oven to 375°F.

Wash the duck, dry it, and make sure to remove any remaining pinfeathers. Pull away and discard any loose pieces of fat. Place the peeled orange inside the cavity. Sprinkle the outside of the duck lightly with salt and garlic powder. Rub into the skin but do not prick the skin. Line the bottom of a roasting pan with tinfoil to catch the grease as it melts. Place the duck on a rack in the roasting pan and cook for 1 hour in the preheated oven. Remove the duck from the oven and allow to cool for 10 to 15 minutes. (Do not turn off the oven.) Split the duck in half using poultry shears or a sharp knife and remove the breastbone. Once you split the duck, you'll find it easy to gently pry the breastbone away from the meat. Drain off any accumulated fat from the roasting pan and replace the duck halves on rack, skin side up. Roast for another 30 to 45 minutes. When done, the skin should be very crisp and browned.

YIELD: *2 to 3 servings.*

# Roast Duck with Orange Sauce

*1 duck (3 ½ to 4 ½ pounds)*
*1 orange, peeled*
*Salt*
*Garlic powder*
*½ cup brown sugar*
*1 tablespoon cornstarch*
*1 cup orange juice*

*1 tablespoon grated orange rind*
*Juice of 1 lemon*
*2 tablespoons orange liqueur*
*(optional)*
*2 oranges, sliced into thin*
*rounds*
*Parsley, for garnish*

Preheat oven to 375°F.

Wash the duck, dry it, and make sure to remove any remaining pinfeathers. Pull away and discard any loose pieces of fat. Place the peeled orange inside the cavity. Sprinkle the outside of the duck lightly with salt and garlic powder. Rub into the skin but do not prick the skin. Line the bottom of a roasting pan with tinfoil to catch the grease as it melts. Place the duck on a rack in the roasting pan and cook for 1 hour in the preheated oven.

In the meantime, mix together the brown sugar and the cornstarch. Place in a saucepan together with the orange juice, orange rind, lemon juice, and orange liqueur. Stir well and bring to a boil. Reduce to a simmer, stirring constantly until mixture loses its cloudiness and thickens slightly.

Remove the duck from the oven and allow to cool for 10 to 15 minutes. (Do not turn off the oven.) Split the duck in half using poultry shears or a sharp knife and remove the breastbone by gently prying the meat away from the bone. Drain off any accumulated fat from the roasting pan and replace the duck halves

on rack, skin side up. Brush the duck with orange sauce and reserve the remaining sauce to serve at the table. Roast for another
30 to 40 minutes. When done, the skin should be very crisp and
browned.

Serve the duck halves surrounded by sliced oranges and garnished with parsley. Pass warm orange sauce in a gravy bowl. This
duck goes very nicely with any rice dish.

YIELD:  *2 to 3 servings.*

*Advice from Mama:*  For a very fancy variation, heat ⅓ cup
orange liqueur in a small saucepan. Place the roast duck halves on
a preheated platter, decorate, and pour heated liqueur over the
duck. Strike a match and light the liqueur in the bottom of the
serving platter. Carry the duck flambé to the dining table to a
chorus of ooohs and aaahs.

*More advice from Mama:*  For an exotic variation, try mixing
together ⅓ cup of honey, ⅓ cup of orange juice, and 1 teaspoon
of curry powder. Salt and pepper the duck to taste as usual. Apply
half of the sweet, spicy mixture to the bird. Roast in preheated
oven as above. Periodically baste the roasting duck with the remaining liquid. This delicious coating on the duck will have you
dreaming of warm nights in Kashmir.

# Roast Goose with Bread and Apple Stuffing

Years ago, when my children were still young teenagers, I an-
nounced to them that I thought I would attempt to make a goose
instead of a turkey for Thanksgiving. They were a little unhappy
about not having turkey, but were willing to try. So I ordered a
fresh goose and on Thanksgiving morning I made the stuffing,
stuffed the goose, did everything right, and placed it in the oven.
When the goose was ready we sat down to a beautiful table and

waited for my husband to start carving. Well, just picture a "sitcom" where no matter what you do you can't cut, slice, or hack that goose. We sharpened our knife—that didn't work. We borrowed a knife from a neighbor—that didn't work. I even tried a cleaver—that was no good. We ate the stuffing and all the trimmings and I gave the goose to our German shepherd dog. Believe it or not, our dog couldn't chew it and finally left it in disgust. The kids were pretty unhappy, although now we all laugh when we retell it at family gatherings. What happened? I still don't know. It was one of those mysteries of cooking that happen to everyone from time to time—you do everything right and everything still comes out wrong.

Back in the old country every housewife was expected to raise her own goose. The goose was kept in a pen and force-fed three times a day. A nice fat goose was proof of a hard-working *balabusta* (housewife). While you are probably not going to raise your own goose, you should try, if possible, to buy a fresh one. To do this, you will probably have to order the goose from your butcher. If you have no local butcher, buy a frozen one two days before cooking and let it defrost inside the refrigerator.

| | |
|---|---|
| *1 loaf white bread* | *¹/₄ teaspoon crushed thyme* |
| *1 goose (6 to 8 pounds)* | *¹/₂ tablespoon kosher salt* |
| *2 tablespoons corn oil* | *2 teaspoons garlic powder* |
| *2 onions, finely chopped* | *2 large McIntosh apples* |
| *2 stalks celery, finely chopped* | *Salt* |

Tear or cut the bread slices into small cubes and leave on a baking sheet overnight to dry. If you don't have enough time, put in a low (250°F) oven for 1½ to 2 hours.

Preheat oven to 375°F.

Wash and dry the goose and pull out any remaining pinfeathers. Heat the corn oil in a skillet and sauté the onions for 5 minutes, until just wilted. Add the celery, thyme, salt, and 1 teaspoon garlic powder. Sauté 2 minutes more and remove from heat. Peel, core, and dice the apples. Combine apples, sautéed onions, celery, and the dried bread cubes in a large bowl and mix well. Stuff this mixture into the cavity of the goose and sew or skewer it closed.

Sprinkle the goose with remaining garlic powder and salt and rub into the skin. Place on a rack in a roasting pan and calculate roasting time at 15 to 20 minutes for each pound (between 2 and 3 hours).

Y IELD:   *6 to 8 servings.*

*Advice from Mama:*   Save the rendered goose fat that remains in the roasting pan. Many people consider goose fat to be even more delicious than schmaltz. Pour it into a jar, cover, and refrigerate. It will keep indefinitely and it is great for frying potatoes, latkes, or in any recipe that calls for schmaltz.

# 8

# MEATS

□ □ □ □ □ □ □ □ □ □ □ □ □ □ □ □ □ □

Today everyone is cutting back on eating meat, but when I was growing up, my father wasn't really satisfied unless we had meat or chicken as a main course for dinner. Sure, there were lots of other kinds of dinners that we did have—dairy dinners, fish dinners, soup dinners—but real dinners, according to my father, and the rest of America, revolved around meat. Of course, our meat dinners were a little different from those of the rest of America. We never had bloody rare steaks, rare roast beef, or even hamburgers that I can remember. While my mother did not keep a kosher home, she and my father were not so assimilated that they could appreciate the very non-Jewish delights of rare meat. In a kosher kitchen bloody beef is forbidden and, by and large, kosher or not, Jews do not eat their meat rare. If you buy from a kosher butcher, which my mother did, the meat has been salted and soaked until every last trace of blood has been removed. This is the kind of meat that lends itself to long, slow, moist cooking, which are the kinds of dishes you will find in this section.

Not all, but most, of my meat recipes call for the less expensive cuts of meat, which will be cooked slowly, for a long time, until they are tender and tasty.

Flanken is a particularly beloved Jewish cut that you will probably only find at a kosher butcher. Flanken are beef short ribs that are cut in one continuous strip, approximately two inches wide, and resembles a kind of fleshy ammunition belt. If you cannot find flanken, by all means substitute an equal amount of short ribs.

Brisket is another delicious cut of beef that is often called for in the Jewish kitchen. The beef brisket is the breast of the animal, like a breast of veal, only it is never sold with the bones still attached. It is very flavorful and is good boiled or pot-roasted.

Most of the meat cuts that are called for in the following recipes are easily interchangeable with other similar cuts. You can make pot roast with brisket, bottom round, top round, eye round, or chuck. So don't worry, buy whatever is on sale in the supermarket or butcher shop.

## Roast Veal

In Europe veal has always been a very popular dish. Many farmers preferred to kill their calves early rather than pay the expense of feeding a steer until it was fully mature. Jews, too, ate veal with relish, but mostly they ate the less expensive cuts. Calf's feet went into making Petcha (page 38), breast of veal was stuffed or potted, and calf's liver and tongue were considered great delicacies. When I was growing up, a roast of veal was for very special occasions, because it was then and still is a very expensive cut. But when I feel like splurging and serving a special main course, roast veal is the dish I serve.

The roast veal is served with a simple pan-juice gravy thickened by the cooked onions, which are pressed through a sieve.

2 tablespoons garlic powder
1 teaspoon kosher salt
1 teaspoon paprika
¼ teaspoon freshly ground
   black pepper
4 to 5 pounds veal shoulder
   roast

2 medium onions, thinly sliced
2 cloves garlic, split in half
1 cup water
Salt to taste

Preheat oven to 375°F.

Mix together the garlic powder, salt, paprika, and black pepper in a small bowl. Rub this mixture all over the veal. Place roast over sliced onions in a roasting pan. Add fresh garlic and water. Cover and roast in a preheated oven for 1½ hours, remove cover and roast for an additional 30 minutes. Turn the temperature up to 475°F for the last 15 minutes, in order to brown the roast.

Remove the veal to a platter. If you would like to have a little gravy, add 1½ cups water to the pan juices and onions in the roasting pan. Cook on top of the stove, over high heat, for about 5 minutes. Taste for seasoning and add salt if necessary. Strain through a sieve, pushing on the onions with the back of a spoon to extract all the juices.

Serve with Oven Roast Potatoes (page 200).

YIELD:   *6 to 8 servings.*

# Potted Breast of Veal

Because this is a very inexpensive cut of veal, my mother made this dish relatively often. For some reason I never understood, she insisted on calling it calf's meat instead of veal. She would kosher it, wash it, season it, and cook it in the oven. She never removed the layer of fat that covered the breast because who knew about cholesterol? These days I carefully cut away whatever fat I can before cooking.

*1 whole breast of veal (3 to 4
    pounds)*
*2 medium onions, sliced*
*6 carrots, peeled and cut into
    bite-size pieces*
*6 cloves garlic, crushed*
*1 teaspoon salt or to taste*

*½ cup ketchup*
*2 bay leaves*
*Enough water to cover the veal
    ¾ of the way*
*4 potatoes, peeled and quartered
    (optional)*

Preheat oven to 375°F.

Use a small, sharp knife to cut away all visible fat from the breast of veal. Place all the ingredients except for the potatoes into a large, heavy pot with a tight-fitting lid. Pour in enough water to cover the breast of veal ¾ of the way up. Cover and bake for 2 hours. Remove cover, add more water if necessary (there should be about 2 inches of liquid), and add the potatoes if desired. Cook uncovered for 45 minutes to 1 hour longer.

Skim all visible fat from the surface, remove bay leaves, taste for seasoning, and serve, or refrigerate overnight and remove congealed fat. Cut through the ribs and reheat before serving. Cut the veal so as to serve 1 rib per person.

YIELD: *6 to 8 servings.*

# Stuffed Breast of Veal

Here we have a kishke stuffing in a breast of veal—scrumptious! I developed the idea for this type of stuffing at my restaurant because almost everyone loves kishke because of the stuffing, and everyone loves the succulence of breast of veal. So the one stuffed inside the other made a perfect marriage. This dish also makes a perfect Passover meal.

1 large whole breast of veal
    (about 4 to 5 pounds)

## Stuffing

1 large onion, finely minced
1/2 cup Schmaltz (rendered
    chicken fat) (page 10) or corn
    oil
3 cups matzo meal

1 teaspoon garlic powder
1/2 teaspoon paprika
1 teaspoon salt or to taste
1 cup water, approximately

## To Cook the Breast of Veal

3 onions, sliced
4 cloves garlic, crushed
2 carrots, peeled and cut into
    pieces

2 teaspoons salt
2 bay leaves
6 cups water

Have your butcher slice open a pocket along the length of the breast of veal, between the meat and the bones. Ask him to remove as much fat as possible. You can also do this yourself using a small, sharp knife.

Sauté the onion in the schmaltz until it is wilted and starting to turn brown. Stir into matzo meal. Add garlic powder, paprika, salt, and just enough water to moisten. Fill the pocket of the veal breast with the stuffing, pushing it in with your fingers. Sew the pocket closed with kitchen twine or wrap around with twine in a few places and tie.

Preheat oven to 375°F.

Place the sliced onions, garlic, carrots, salt, bay leaves, and water in a large roasting pan. Place the stuffed breast of veal on top and bake for 2 hours. Remove cover and cook for 1 hour more, or until meat is fork tender at the thickest point. If you have any doubts, cook 30 minutes longer. More cooking is better with breast of veal because it will just be more tender. Remove breast to a large platter. Strain the gravy, skim away any visible fat, press the carrots through the strainer into the gravy to thicken it, and serve with veal.

To serve, cut the veal so as to serve 1 rib per person.

YIELD:   *6 to 8 servings.*

# Flanken

This is a dish that sounds as though it might be impossibly bland but is actually very tasty. It makes a satisfying, cozy winter meal or whenever you're sick of *nouvelle,* Chinese, and pizza. If you prepare it for your father or your *zaideh* (grandfather), he'll be so grateful he'll put you back in the will—he may even add your boyfriend who isn't Jewish.

Isaac Bashevis Singer, the famous Jewish writer, became a vegetarian when he was twenty and has remained one all his life. Still he says, "The only thing that tempts me now is *flanken.*"

*4 pounds lean flanken (or 4
   pounds short ribs)
Water to cover
2 onions, sliced
4 cloves garlic, crushed*

*1 teaspoon salt
1 carrot, cut in half
2 bay leaves
Horseradish (for serving)*

Place flanken in a large saucepan. Add enough water to cover by 2 inches, then add the remaining ingredients. Bring to a boil, lower heat to a simmer, and cook at a low simmer for 2½ to 3 hours or until meat is fork tender. If it feels slightly rubbery when pinched, it needs additional cooking time.

Remove flanken from broth and serve with horseradish. Strain the broth and reserve 1 cup for reheating any leftover flanken and save rest for another use. It freezes perfectly, makes an excellent beef broth, or makes a good base for mushroom gravy.

YIELD: *4 servings.*

*Advice from Mama:* For a sweet variation (though not with any sweetener), try the following preparation. Add 1 can of butter beans, along with the liquid from the container. Cut up 4 carrots into inch-thick chunks. Simmer as above, keeping lid ajar in latter stages to let pot liquor cook down to a thick juice. You'll find that the butter beans and carrots combine into a deliciously sweet stew, alongside the tender flanken.

# Brisket in Natural Gravy

This brisket is better if prepared a day ahead and refrigerated overnight so that the congealed fat can be easily removed. The brisket and the strained pan juices should be reheated together.

*4 to 5 pounds brisket*
*4 medium onions, sliced*
*4 carrots, peeled and cut into
   2-inch chunks*
*2 bay leaves*

*6 cloves garlic, crushed*
*2 teaspoons salt*
*¼ teaspoon freshly ground
   black pepper*
*4 cups water, approximately*

Preheat oven to 375°F.

Place the brisket, together with the onions, carrots, bay leaves, garlic, salt, and pepper, in a Dutch oven or heavy roasting pan with a tightly fitting cover. Add enough water to just cover the meat. Cover tightly and cook in a preheated oven for 2½ to 3 hours, until the brisket is fork tender. Remove the brisket to a platter. Strain the pan juices and discard the carrots and onions, or save and serve as a vegetable side dish. Reheat the pan juices in a saucepan. Slice the brisket and serve the pan juices in a gravy boat. Serve with kasha varnishkes or mashed potatoes. The leftover brisket makes wonderful sandwiches.

YIELD:    *10 to 12 servings.*

# Meat Tzimmes

"Don't make a big tzimmes!" my mother used to say whenever I would start complaining about something unimportant. But when she made a tzimmes, it was delicious. Carrots are the heart of tzimmes—they give a sweetness to the dish, which is traditionally eaten at the Rosh Hashana table, forecasting a sweet new year. Carrots have always been a staple in Jewish cooking, perhaps because the ancient Hebrews thought they were an aphrodisiac! *Oi vey!* I have a headache. . . .

Tzimmes made without meat is parve and can be served as a side dish with any meal (page 202). In the following recipe the meat and vegetables together make a perfect meal-in-one. Meat tzimmes is especially appropriate to serve for the Jewish New Year because its sweetness holds a promise for a sweet new year and its opulent richness is an appropriate mark of this special occasion.

*3 to 4 pounds brisket*

*8 carrots, scraped and cut into large pieces*

*3 yams or sweet potatoes, peeled and quartered*

*3 potatoes, peeled and quartered*

*12 pitted prunes (cut in half if they are very large)*

*1 small onion, diced*

*2 cloves garlic, crushed*

*3 cups orange juice*

*3 cups water*

*1/4 cup orange liqueur*

*2 tablespoons brown sugar*

*2 teaspoons salt*

Preheat oven to 375°F.

Place brisket in a heavy Dutch oven. Arrange carrots, yams or sweet potatoes, potatoes, prunes, onion, and garlic around the brisket. Mix together the orange juice, water, orange liqueur, brown sugar, and salt, and pour over the brisket and vegetables. Cover and bake for 2½ to 3 hours. Remove cover, add a little more water if it looks too dry, and bake for another 30 to 45 minutes, or until almost all the liquid has cooked away and the vegetables have glazed. Remove the meat, slice and serve with vegetables.

YIELD:   *6 to 8 servings.*

# Glazed Brisket

I was once served this at a buffet party and thought it was one of the best, tastiest, and most unusual main courses I had ever been served at a party. I was happy to get the recipe and now I'm delighted to pass it on.

*4 to 5 pounds brisket*
*1 onion, thinly sliced*
*3 cloves garlic, crushed*
*3 to 4 cups water, or enough to*
   *cover the meat*

*½ cup brown sugar*
*1 cup apricot jam or plum*
   *preserves*

Place brisket, onion, garlic, and water in a large ovenproof casserole with a tight-fitting lid. Cover and simmer for 1½ to 2 hours, or until the meat is almost fork tender. Remove the beef and strain the broth. Reserve ½ cup of strained broth and save the rest for another purpose.

Mix the sugar with the ½ cup of broth until it is dissolved, then stir in apricot jam or plum preserves. Mix well.

Preheat oven to 375°F.

Put the brisket back in the pot, pour apricot mix over it and bake, uncovered, for an additional 45 minutes to 1 hour. Remove to platter and dribble over it any juices that are left in the casserole. Let stand for 10 minutes, then slice and serve.

YIELD: *6 to 8 servings.*

# Sweet and Sour Beef (Essig Flaisch)

My mother never made this dish. She came from the Ukraine and the marriage of sweet and sour flavors was alien to her. The taste for sweet and sour flavoring with meat dishes reflects much more of a Polish influence. Over the years several of my customers would ask me to make it, so I took a little bit of one recipe and a little bit from another until it came out delicious.

*3 to 4 pounds brisket or chuck*
*3 medium onions, sliced thin*
*1 teaspoon salt*
*¼ teaspoon pepper*
*2 cloves garlic, crushed*
*1 bay leaf*

*4 cups boiling water,*
*approximately*
*2 tablespoons lemon juice*
*3 tablespoons brown sugar*
*3 gingersnaps, crumbled*
*(optional)*

Preheat oven to 375°F.

Place meat in casserole. Add all the ingredients except water, lemon juice, brown sugar, and gingersnaps. Pour in water to come up ¾ of the way. Cover the casserole and bake in oven or simmer on top of stove for 2½ to 3 hours, or until tender. Remove from oven or heat, add lemon juice, brown sugar, and gingersnaps. Stir and taste. If you like it sweeter, add more sugar; if you like it more tart, add more lemon juice. Slice and serve with pan juices.

YIELD: *6 to 8 servings.*

# German-Jewish Pot Roast
# (Sauerbraten)

Plan ahead when you want to make this dish. The special piquant sweet and sour flavor of sauerbraten comes from a lengthy marinating in vinegar, sugar, water, and spices. The meat is marinated for up to 3 days, acquiring in the process deep flavor and a particular tenderness.

*2 onions, sliced*
*4 bay leaves*
*8 whole peppercorns*
*1 tablespoon salt*
*1/4 cup sugar*
*1/4 cup red wine vinegar*
*2 cups water, enough to cover*
*  meat halfway*

*3 to 4 pounds bottom round,*
*  brisket, or chuck*
*1/4 cup brown sugar*
*1/4 cup raisins*
*8 pitted prunes*
*1/4 teaspoon ground ginger*
*1 teaspoon potato starch*

Place onions, bay leaves, peppercorns, salt, sugar, vinegar, and water in a deep glass or ceramic bowl. Mix well, until sugar is dissolved. Place meat in marinade, pierce it all over with a long-pronged fork, and turn it in marinade several times. Cover with plastic wrap and refrigerate for 2 to 3 days. Turn meat in marinade at least twice a day.

Preheat oven to 450°F.

Remove the meat and place it in a heavy Dutch oven. Strain and reserve the marinade. Add all the onions to the meat and about 3 tablespoons of the marinade. Bake, uncovered, for 15 to 20 minutes, until meat browns.

Add 2 cups of marinade and as much water as necessary to cover the meat halfway. Reduce oven temperature to 375°F. Cover tightly and cook for 2½ to 3 hours, until tender.

Remove meat to a serving platter and strain the pan juices. Replace in pot and add brown sugar, raisins, prunes, and ginger. If you wish to thicken the pan juices, remove ¼ cup of liquid from the pot and dissolve the potato starch in it. Return to pot and heat gently on top of the stove, until thickened. Do not boil.

Slice the pot roast, pour the pan juices over it, and serve.

YIELD: *6 to 8 servings.*

# Pot Roast (Gedempte Flaisch)

Make this the day before you want to serve it. This is a great "freezer to oven" dish, or one that is made several days ahead of when you need it. The longer it hangs around, it seems, the better it tastes. I love eating this pot roast with kasha varnishkes. In fact, I can make a meal of just kasha varnishkes with pot roast gravy. Save the pot roast for sandwiches.

*2½ to 3 pounds bottom round, eye of the round, or brisket*
*2 medium onions, sliced*
*4 carrots, sliced*
*6 cloves garlic, crushed*
*2 teaspoons salt, or to taste*

*2 bay leaves*
*1 cup ketchup*
*3 cups water, or enough to cover meat halfway*
*4 potatoes, quartered*

Preheat oven to 375°F.

Place the meat, onions, carrots, garlic, salt, bay leaves, ketchup, and enough water to cover the meat halfway up in a Dutch oven or a heavy pot with a tight-fitting lid. Cook in a preheated oven, tightly covered, for 2 hours. After 2 hours, add potatoes and as much water as necessary to cover meat halfway. Cover and continue cooking for another 40 to 50 minutes, or until meat is tender and the potatoes are cooked through. Let cool at room temperature, then cover and refrigerate overnight. The next day, remove all congealed fat, remove the bay leaves, slice the meat, reheat and serve. I always slice the meat cold because it is much easier to get nice slices, then I replace it in the gravy, cover the pot, reheat on top of stove over low heat for 30 minutes (until potatoes are heated through).

YIELD:  *6 servings.*

# Polish-Jewish Pot Roast

I call this "Polisher"-style pot roast because anything that's not "Litvak"-style and is sweetened was automatically put in that category by my mother. It's true that some Polish-style Jewish foods often contain sugar or raisins (or both). Polish stuffed cabbage always has both sugar and raisins added, and gefilte fish Polish-style is made with sugar. However, even though we tended to look down our noses at "Polisher"-style cooking, this pot roast is extremely delicious no matter what we call it.

This pot roast is best made the day before you want to eat it. This allows you to remove all the congealed fat, and the flavor improves with the waiting.

*4- to 5-pound brisket or bottom*
*round*
*¹/4 cup brown sugar*
*¹/2 cup ketchup*
*¹/4 cup vinegar*

*1 tablespoon salt*
*2 cloves garlic, crushed*
*2 onions, sliced*
*4 carrots, cut into bite-size pieces*
*2 cups water*

Preheat oven to 375°F.

Place all the above ingredients in a heavy ovenproof casserole with a tight-fitting lid. Cover and bake in oven for 2½ to 3 hours.

Remove, let cool, and refrigerate overnight. Remove all the congealed fat. Slice meat, place in gravy, and reheat on top of stove.

YIELD:  *6 to 8 servings.*

# Beef Stew in Wine

This may not sound very Jewish, but don't say that to a French Jew! Any way you look at it, this is a delicious stew and a great buffet dish. You can easily make it a day ahead, as it will only taste better.

*3 to 4 pounds lean chuck or bottom round, cut into cubes about 1 1/2 inches square*
*1 large onion, diced fine*
*6 cloves garlic, crushed*
*1 tablespoon salt*
*3 bay leaves*
*8 carrots, peeled and cut into bite-size pieces*

*2 cups dry red wine*
*Water to cover*
*4 russet or Idaho potatoes, peeled and cut into bite-size pieces*
*12 small white onions, peeled and left whole*
*Flour to thicken*
*1 package frozen peas*

Preheat oven to 375°F.

Put meat, diced onion, garlic, salt, bay leaves, carrots, and red wine into a Dutch oven. Add enough water for the liquid to cover the solid ingredients. Cover and bake for 2 hours. Add the potatoes and onions and cook 30 minutes longer. Dissolve flour in a little cold water and add with frozen peas. Stir in to blend and cook for another 10 minutes to thicken.

Serve immediately or reheat the next day.

YIELD:  *6 to 8 servings.*

*Advice from Mama:*   I used to use only russet or Idaho potatoes. Lately, I like to get little new potatoes, cut them in half or thirds without even peeling them.

# Beef and Cabbage Stew

This recipe probably originated in Poland because of the sweet and sour taste. The use of cabbage in meat dishes of all kinds is, of course, common throughout Eastern Europe.

| | |
|---|---|
| *3 to 5 pounds brisket or 3 to 4 pounds chuck* | *3 tablespoons corn oil* |
| *2 teaspoons salt* | *1 large onion, diced* |
| *Water to cover* | *3 tablespoons brown sugar* |
| *1 large green cabbage* | *3 tablespoons red wine vinegar* |
| | *1 clove garlic, crushed* |

Cut the meat into 1-inch chunks. Place the meat into a heavy ovenproof casserole or Dutch oven, then add salt and water to cover. Cover with a tight-fitting lid and simmer for approximately 1½ hours or until meat is almost tender. Stir occasionally and skim off any fat that rises to the surface.

Meanwhile, cut cabbage into quarters. Remove bruised outer leaves and cut away the hard core. Shred the cabbage quarters. Heat the oil in a large frying pan. Add the onion and cook, stirring, until onion turns golden. Add shredded cabbage and continue cooking, stirring frequently until cabbage begins to brown. Mix together the sugar, vinegar, and garlic. Stir into the cabbage.

Preheat oven to 350°F.

Add the cabbage to the meat. Stir and cover the casserole. Place in oven and continue cooking until meat is very tender, 45 minutes to 1 hour. Remove from oven and check for seasoning. If the stew is too watery, add a little flour (2 tablespoons) dissolved in ¼ cup cold water and cook for 5 to 10 minutes until it thickens.

YIELD: *6 to 8 servings.*

*Advice from Mama:* Add some peeled and quartered carrots and potatoes at the same time you add the cabbage. These add extra flavor and variety.

# Short Ribs Stew

To my surprise I have found that many people don't know what to do with short ribs. Here, then, is the answer. Make a stew with them and it will be better than any other beef stew you have ever tasted. My mother always said that short ribs had more *tam* (taste) than other cuts of beef, and, of course, she was right. You know the old saying, don't you: "The closer to the bone, the sweeter the meat."

8 to 12 short ribs, depending on their size
2 medium onions, cut into chunks
6 to 8 carrots, peeled and cut into chunks
4 cloves garlic, crushed
2 teaspoons salt

1/2 teaspoon freshly ground black pepper
1 1/2 cups ketchup
2 cups water, or enough to just cover
2 bay leaves
4 potatoes, peeled and quartered
1 package frozen peas

Preheat oven to 375°F.

Place all the ingredients except potatoes and peas in a large ovenproof casserole. Cover and bake for 2 hours. Then add potatoes, cover, and cook for 1 more hour. Remove from oven and stir in peas. Let stand 5 minutes, skim off excess fat, and serve.

This is good made a day ahead. Refrigerate overnight, remove all the congealed fat, reheat and serve.

YIELD: *6 to 8 servings.*

# Short Ribs with Sauerkraut

*2 large onions, sliced thin*
*¼ cup corn oil*
*8 to 12 short ribs (depending on size)*
*or*
*3 to 4 pounds chuck, cut into cubes*

*2 cloves garlic, crushed*
*1 teaspoon salt*
*¼ teaspoon pepper*
*1 cup water*
*1½ to 2 pounds sauerkraut, rinsed and drained*
*1 bay leaf*

Preheat oven to 350°F.

Sauté the onions in the corn oil until light brown. Drain and discard the oil. Place the beef, together with onions, garlic, salt, pepper, and water, in a large ovenproof casserole. Cover and cook for 2 hours. Then add sauerkraut and bay leaf and bake for 1 hour more, or until meat is very tender. Discard bay leaf and serve.

YIELD:   *4 to 6 servings.*

# Mama's Famous Meat Loaf

Everybody who's eaten my meat loaf in my home or my restaurant has begged me for my recipe. And for a long time I held back, but now I say, you can buy my cookbook, it will be in there.

Whenever I make meat loaf, I make two. One for now and one for later. Sometimes I freeze the second one for another dinner, sometimes I just keep it in the refrigerator to make great sandwiches. This recipe makes 2 meat loaves, each large enough to feed 4 to 6 people.

*4 pounds ground round or very lean chuck*
*1 large onion, finely minced*

*1 tablespoon salt or to taste*
*¼ to ½ teaspoon black pepper*
*3 large eggs*

*2 to 3 cloves garlic, crushed*
*1 can Campbell's tomato soup*
*½ can water*

*1 cup matzo meal*
*3 tablespoons ketchup*

Preheat oven to 375°F.

In a large mixing bowl combine all the ingredients except matzo meal and ketchup and mix well. The only way to do this properly is to use your hands. So roll up your sleeves, give your hands a good washing, and plunge in, kneading and mixing until everything is well blended. Add the matzo meal and repeat.

Divide the mixture into two bread pans and spread ketchup on top of each meat loaf. Bake for 1 hour.

Y I E L D :  *2 meat loaves.*

## Meatballs in Tomato Sauce

*2 pounds ground chuck or*
  *ground round*
*1 medium onion, finely minced*
*½ cup bread crumbs*
*2 cloves garlic, crushed*
*1 teaspoon freshly ground black*
  *pepper*

*2 teaspoons salt or to taste*
*1 egg*
*¼ cup water*
*2 tablespoons corn oil*
*Tomato Sauce (page 170)*

In a large mixing bowl combine the ground meat, onion, bread crumbs, garlic, freshly ground black pepper, salt, and egg. Mix with your hands, and add just enough water to make a moist mixture that still holds together. Mix until everything is well blended. Shape the mixture into small, oval patties and sauté in hot corn oil until browned on both sides. Discard the oil.

Heat tomato sauce and add the sautéed meatballs. Simmer gently, uncovered, for 30 minutes. Serve with egg noodles or your favorite pasta.

Y I E L D :  *4 to 6 servings.*

# Tomato Sauce

I jokingly call this Jewish-style tomato sauce because I don't use any basil or oregano. But if you want an Italian flavor, then add a teaspoon each of these herbs and you'll have a delicious sauce for pasta or lasagna.

*1 medium onion, diced fine*
*2 tablespoons butter, margarine,*
  *or corn oil*
*4 cloves garlic, crushed*
*1 32-ounce can crushed*
  *tomatoes*
*1 can tomato paste*

*2 bay leaves*
*3 teaspoons sugar (optional)*
*1 teaspoon salt (optional)*
*¹/₄ teaspoon freshly ground*
  *black pepper*
*2 tablespoons minced parsley*

In a large saucepan sauté the onion in butter, margarine, or oil until it is slightly browned. Add the garlic and sauté 1 minute longer. Add the remaining ingredients and simmer for 30 minutes. Discard bay leaves and taste for seasoning.

YIELD:  *4 to 6 cups.*

# Cholent

The best way to describe cholent is as a kind of Jewish cassoulet. This ancient dish goes back to biblical times and is traditionally served in Orthodox Jewish homes on the Sabbath, a day on which no cooking is permitted. The housewife would put it in the oven as late as possible before sundown on Friday evening, where it was left to cook at the lowest possible temperature until midday dinner on Saturday. In the days before households had their own ovens, each family would carry its cholent pot to the village baker to be retrieved the following day.

Because of the long cooking necessary, cholent is the perfect make-ahead dish. Serve it hot right out of the oven, or warm, or even at room temperature.

*2 cups dried lima beans*
*3 medium onions, peeled and*
  *diced*
*¼ cup Schmaltz (rendered*
  *chicken fat) (page 10) or corn*
  *oil*
*6 cloves garlic, crushed*
*2 tablespoons kosher salt*

*½ teaspoon freshly ground*
  *black pepper*
*¼ cup barley*
*3 or 4 large russet or Idaho*
  *potatoes, peeled and quartered*
*3 pounds of brisket, short ribs,*
  *or flanken*
*Water*

Soak lima beans in water to cover for 4 hours or overnight. Preheat oven to 350°F.

Sauté the onions in schmaltz or oil in the bottom of a heavy stockpot or Dutch oven large enough to hold all the ingredients listed above and leave room for beans and barley to expand. Cook, stirring, until onions begins to brown, add garlic, salt, and pepper and cook 1 minute more. Remove half the mixture and reserve. Drain the lima beans and place them in the bottom of the pot on top of the sautéed onions. Sprinkle on barley and layer on the potatoes with the reserved onions. Place the meat over all. Add enough water to cover the meat by 2 inches. Cover the pot very tightly with a layer of tinfoil and a lid on top. Bake for 2 hours. Reduce oven heat to 250°F or lowest possible setting and cook for another 4 hours. Check about halfway through baking time to see if it is not too dry. If all the liquid has been absorbed, add about 2 cups of water.

YIELD: *6 to 8 servings.*

*Advice from Mama:*   If you own a Crockpot, you might try using it for this recipe. It should work very well.

# Kasha Cholent

3 medium onions, diced
1/4 cup vegetable oil or Schmaltz
   (rendered chicken fat) (page
   10)
3 to 4 pounds brisket or 6 flanken
2 cups dried lima beans (soaked in
   water overnight)

4 cloves garlic, crushed
2 tablespoons salt
2 cups kasha (whole buckweat
   groats are preferable, medium
   are okay, too)
6 cups water

Preheat oven to 350°F.

Sauté the onions in oil or schmaltz until they are lightly browned. Place the onions, meat, lima beans, garlic, and salt into a large Dutch oven. Place the kasha on top and pour the water over everything. Cover tightly and bake for 3 to 4 hours or until meat is very tender. Check every hour to see if cholent is too dry. Add hot water, 1/2 cup at a time, if necessary. When meat is tender, remove and slice. Arrange on a platter and surround with the other cholent ingredients. Can be served hot or warm.

YIELD:   *6 to 8 servings.*

# Corned Beef with Vegetables

I find that most corned beef purchased at the supermarket is very good. When I'm in doubt because I'm not familiar with the brand, I ask the butcher in the meat department to point out the brand that he thinks is consistently the best.

3 to 4 pounds lean corned beef
5 to 6 carrots, scraped and
   halved or quartered
3 parsnips, scraped and cut in
   half lengthwise

2 medium heads green cabbage,
   trimmed of outer leaves and
   quartered
6 large potatoes, peeled and cut
   into thirds

*8 small white onions, peeled and*   *4 ears corn on the cob, shucked*
   *left whole*                       *and cut into thirds*

Place corned beef in a very large pot and cover with water by several inches. Bring to a boil and reduce heat to a simmer. Simmer for 2½ to 3 hours, until meat is fork tender. If you're not sure, remove from water, slice a little piece and try it. If the meat has a rubbery texture, it needs at least a half hour longer cooking time. (If you cook it for another half hour and it's still rubbery, take it out and bring it back to the butcher, while you go out for Chinese.) When the meat is tender remove from water and keep it warm. Put all the vegetables, except the corn, in the water and cook until potatoes are done. Add the corn and cook 5 minutes longer.

Slice the corned beef and arrange on a platter. Surround with vegetables and pour over a little of the broth to keep everything moist. Discard the remaining broth. Serve with horseradish or mustard and plenty of good rye bread.

Y I E L D :   *6 to 8 servings.*

# Calves' Tongues with
# Horseradish Sauce

❧

Jews have always looked upon tongue as a delicacy. Beef tongue is usually pickled or smoked because it has a stronger taste, but for fresh, delicious flavor, calf's tongue is worth seeking out. It's even worth it to badger your butcher to special-order them for you. If he can only get them frozen, that's okay. One piece of advice, though: don't tell your children what it is—even if they beg you.

*4 fresh calves' tongues, each
  weighing about 1 pound
2 onions, sliced
½ teaspoon freshly ground
  black pepper
2 bay leaves
4 cloves garlic, crushed*

*1 tablespoon vinegar
Water to cover
2 tablespoons potato starch
3 tablespoons bottled white
  horseradish
Fresh parsley, minced*

Rinse the tongues under cold running water and place them in a pot large enough to hold them. Add the onions, pepper, bay leaves, garlic, vinegar, and enough water to cover. Bring water to a boil, then reduce heat. Cover and simmer until almost fork tender, about 1 to 1½ hours. Remove tongues from cooking liquid and plunge into cold water to cool. Cut away the root end of each tongue. Slit tongue casing down the length of the tongue and peel away the casing.

Strain the cooking liquid and return 4 cups of stock to the pot. Dissolve potato starch in ¼ cup cold water and stir into the stock. Heat gently (do not boil) until thickened. This will only take a minute or two. Stir in horseradish and taste for seasoning. Slice the tongues, starting from the tip, cutting at a slight angle. The slices should be no more than ¼ inch thick. Pour some of the gravy over the sliced tongues and serve the rest in a gravy boat. Garnish with minced parsley.

YIELD: *6 to 8 servings.*

# Sweet and Sour Calves' Tongues

My mother always potted the calves' tongues the same way she did her Breast of Veal (page 154). When she could get them, she would use Lamb Tongues (page 179), which are very small and delicious. But she never made a sweet and sour tongue. My restaurant customers frequently asked for it, so I devised this recipe and found that I enjoyed it as much as they did. I hope you like it, too.

| | |
|---|---|
| 4 calves' tongues | 2 bay leaves |
| 2 onions, sliced | 4 cloves garlic, crushed |
| 1/2 teaspoon freshly ground | 1 tablespoon vinegar |
|    black pepper | Water to cover |

Rinse the tongues under cold running water and place them in a pot large enough to hold them. Add the onions, pepper, bay leaves, garlic, vinegar, and enough water to cover. Bring water to a boil, then reduce heat. Cover and simmer for 1 hour. Remove tongue from the cooking liquid and plunge into cold water to cool. Cut away the root end of each tongue. Slit tongue casing down the length of the tongue and peel away the casing.

Preheat oven to 375°F.

Place the tongue in an ovenproof casserole or Dutch oven and add the following ingredients:

| | |
|---|---|
| 1 onion, minced | 12 pitted prunes |
| 2 cloves garlic, crushed | 1/2 cup raisins |
| 1/2 cup ketchup | 1 1/2 cups water, or enough to |
| 1/4 cup brown sugar |    cover the tongues 3/4 of the |
| 1/4 cup wine vinegar |    way |
| 1 teaspoon salt | |

Cover and bake for 1 to 1 1/2 hours. Remove the tongues from the sauce, slice them on the diagonal into 1/4-inch-thick slices. Arrange slices on a platter and cover with gravy, prunes, and raisins. Serve extra gravy on the side.

YIELD: *6 to 8 servings.*

# Sautéed Calf's Liver

2 medium onions, sliced
4 tablespoons corn oil
¼ cup flour
1 teaspoon salt

¼ teaspoon pepper
4 slices calf's liver (¼ inch thick), kosher is best if available

Sauté the onions in oil in a large skillet. Mix the flour with the salt and pepper and place in a shallow plate. Dredge the liver in seasoned flour and set aside. When onions start to brown, push them to the side of the skillet. Turn up the heat and fry each liver slice, 3 to 4 minutes on one side and 2 to 3 minutes on the other. If you like it a little rare inside, decrease the cooking time by a minute or two. Remove to a platter and continue until all the liver is fried. Remove the browned onions with a slotted spoon and place over the liver.

I like to serve liver with either mashed potatoes or egg noodles and to put some of the onions on those as well.

YIELD: *2 to 4 servings.*

# Roast Stuffed Leg of Lamb

If you love lamb as much as I do, then this dish will satisfy your cravings. The boned, stuffed leg of lamb serves more people than a regular leg of lamb and is much easier to carve and serve. I love this dish served with oven-roasted potatoes and green peas or creamed spinach. Also, a dish of mint jelly served with the lamb is a must.

Do keep in mind that leg of lamb is not considered a kosher cut of meat, and you may wish to substitute a boned shoulder of lamb.

*1 whole leg of lamb (4 to 5*
   *pounds), boned and butterflied*
*Bread Stuffing (page 146)*
   *(substitute thyme for poultry*
   *seasoning)*
*2 teaspoons salt*
*1 tablespoon garlic powder*

*1 teaspoon dried thyme*
*1/4 teaspoon freshly ground*
   *black pepper*
*1 medium onion, thinly sliced*
*1 1/2 cups water*
*2 tablespoons flour*

Preheat oven to 425°F.

Ask butcher to bone and butterfly the leg of lamb. Save the bones. Spread the bread stuffing evenly over the lamb. Roll up and tie in four places with butcher's twine. Mix together the salt, garlic powder, thyme, and black pepper. Rub this mixture all over the lamb.

Place in roasting pan, uncovered, together with the bones, sliced onion, and 1/4 cup water. Roast for 20 minutes. Reduce heat to 375°F and cook for an additional hour. Remove the lamb and discard the bones. Add flour to the pan juices and cook, stirring, for 5 minutes on top of the stove over medium heat. Add the remaining 1 1/4 cups water, bring to a boil, and cook for 5 minutes to make a gravy. Strain the gravy, skim the fat, and taste for seasoning. Serve with the sliced lamb and mint jelly.

YIELD: *6 to 10 servings.*

*Advice from Mama:* If you like your lamb still pink inside, roast for 10 minutes at 425°F, then 45 minutes at 375°F.

# Lamb Kebabs

These taste best if left to marinate overnight.

*3- to 4-pound shank half of leg
  of lamb or shoulder
1 cup dry red wine
¼ cup corn oil
¼ cup red wine vinegar
1 teaspoon dried oregano
1 teaspoon salt
¼ teaspoon freshly ground
  black pepper
6 cloves garlic, crushed*

*2 to 3 bay leaves
¼ cup minced parsley
2 Bermuda onions, cut into
  eighths
12 large mushrooms, stemmed
2 green peppers, cored, seeded,
  and cut into 2-inch chunks
4 large tomatoes, quartered, or 1
  pint cherry tomatoes*

Have butcher bone lamb and cut into 1½-inch cubes. Combine wine, oil, vinegar, oregano, salt, pepper, garlic, bay leaves, and parsley in a large bowl. Mix well and add the cubed lamb. Mix again to make sure all lamb pieces are well exposed to the marinade. Marinate for at least 6 hours or overnight, but no more than 18 hours because the wine vinegar may overwhelm the flavor of the lamb.

Remove lamb pieces from the marinade and add the vegetables. Marinate vegetables for 1 hour. Arrange lamb pieces and vegetables on skewers, alternating and distributing pieces evenly. Grill over hot coals for about 8 to 10 minutes or in oven broiler for 12 to 15 minutes. This is for well-done lamb; if you prefer lamb a little pink inside, reduce the cooking time by a few minutes.

Serve with Rice Pilaf (page 94) and a green salad.

Y I E L D :  *6 to 8 servings.*

# Potted Lamb Tongues

You will have to ask your butcher to order these for you. Figure on one to two tongues per person. It's hard to fool the kids with this one because these tongues are served whole, but, then, why bother? Let them eat hamburgers and save this for adult company. It is a great dinner party dish and has never failed to be popular with my guests.

| | |
|---|---|
| *6 to 8 lamb tongues* | *4 carrots, scraped and diced* |
| *1 tablespoon salt* | *3 cloves garlic, crushed* |
| *½ cup ketchup* | *1 bay leaf* |
| *3 cups water* | *1 teaspoon salt* |
| *1 large onion, diced* | |

Rinse the tongues under cold running water. Place them in a large pot with enough water to cover, add salt, and bring to a boil. Reduce heat and simmer for 30 minutes. Remove tongues from the cooking liquid and plunge into cold water to cool. Discard the water they were cooked in. Cut away the root ends of each tongue. Slit tongue casing down the length of the tongue and peel away the casing.

Preheat oven to 375°F.

Place the prepared tongues and all the other ingredients in a large, heavy pot with a tight-fitting lid. Pour in enough water to just barely cover the lamb tongues. Cover and bake for 1 hour. Remove cover, add more water if necessary (there should be about 2 inches of liquid). Cook, uncovered, for 45 minutes to 1 hour longer.

Skim all visible fat from the surface, remove bay leaf, taste for seasoning, and serve.

YIELD:  *4 to 6 servings.*

# 9

# STUFFED VEGETABLES

□ □ □ □ □ □ □ □ □ □ □ □ □ □ □ □ □ □ □ □ □ □ □ □ □ □ □ □ □ □ □ □ □

The Greeks *stuff their* grape leaves, the Italians stuff arti-
chokes, Middle Easterners stuff zucchini, the Hungarians
stuff peppers, and the Russians and Poles stuff cabbage leaves.
Since there aren't too many more vegetables that lend themselves
to being stuffed and cooked, I've selected the two most familiar to
me—peppers and cabbage.

Most Polish Jews love their stuffed cabbage on the sweet side,
cooked with lots of brown sugar and raisins. The Russian Jew likes
his stuffed cabbage very spicy. I like it best sweet and sour, more
on the spicy side. After you make it once you can change the
seasonings to suit yourself.

Incidentally, you may be interested to know that stuffed cabbage
rolls have a rather musical history. Rimsky-Korsakov and Mus-
sorgsky were very partial to the sweet and sour taste of stuffed
cabbage rolls. And, according to Gertrude Stein, the dancers of the
Diaghilev ballet practically lived on it.

# Stuffed Cabbage

One reason why poor Jews and Russian peasants survived in hard times is that no matter what the shortage of other foods, there were usually plenty of cabbages, onions, beets, and kasha. Stuffed cabbage, also known as goluptsi, holishkes, holopches, praakes, sarmaale, depending on where in Eastern Europe you came from, was one very popular method of making a little bit of meat go a long way. The 2 pounds of meat called for in my recipe reflect the prosperity of the New World over the more frugal proportions in Old World recipes. But you can adjust this recipe to your own taste by increasing the amount of rice and decreasing the amount of meat. You can try other grains, such as barley, brown rice, and even kasha. This is a great recipe for experimentation, since you can't really make much of a mistake.

This dish is a particular favorite of my niece, Debbie. In fact, when she was very young, she said to my mother, "Grandma, please give your recipe to my mother before you die." She laughs now, because, as she says, "Give it to my mother! That would have been a waste of time." My sister never was very good in the kitchen except for cleaning.

½ *cup long-grained white rice*
2 *pounds lean ground chuck or round*
1 *large onion, diced fine*
3 *cloves garlic, finely diced or put through a garlic press*

1 *tablespoon salt*
¼ *teaspoon freshly ground black pepper*

## Cooking Sauce

2 *cups ketchup*
½ *cup brown sugar*
4 *cloves garlic, crushed*
1 *tablespoon salt*

2 *cups water*

2 *large heads green cabbage*
3 *large onions, chopped*

Parboil rice for 7 to 10 minutes. Drain and mix with ground meat, finely diced onion, garlic, salt, and pepper. The best way to do this is to knead it with your hands.

Mix together the ketchup, brown sugar, garlic, salt, and water and set aside.

Bring a very large pot of water to a boil. Use a small, sharp knife to cut the cores out of the cabbages. Boil each cabbage for 10 minutes. Remove and cool under cold running water. Drain carefully. Peel away the large outer leaves until you get to inner cabbage leaves that look too small to stuff. You want to have about 26 large, stuffable leaves. Reserve large outer leaves for stuffing, chop small inner cabbage leaves into chunks.

Place half the cut-up cabbage together with half the chopped onions on the bottom of a large, heavy Dutch oven or roasting pan.

Preheat oven to 375°F.

Stuff the large cabbage leaves by placing a spoonful of the meat mixture in the center of each leaf. Fold over the ribbed end of the leaf, then fold over the two sides and roll up. Place each cabbage roll, fold side down, onto the chopped cabbage and onions in the Dutch oven. When the cabbage leaves are all stuffed and packed into the pot (they will be in one or two layers depending on the pot size), place the rest of the cut-up cabbage and onion over the cabbage rolls. Pour sauce over all, cover tightly, and bake for 1 ½ to 2 hours, until the cabbage is very tender and the sauce has darkened. Place the cabbage rolls in a deep serving platter and cover with sauce. Serve with boiled potatoes or just on its own with good rye bread.

This is delicious served right away, but even better reheated the following day, and the day after.

YIELD:  *6 to 8 servings.*

# Vegetarian Stuffed Cabbage

♥

| | |
|---|---|
| 2 large heads cabbage | 1/4 teaspoon pepper |
| 4 cups cooked rice | 2 cups ketchup |
| 1 large onion, minced | 1/4 cup brown sugar |
| 2 cups carrots, cooked and diced | 3 cloves garlic |
| 1/2 pound mushrooms, sliced | 1 teaspoon salt |
| 2 teaspoons salt | 4 cups water |
| 1 teaspoon garlic powder | 2 medium onions, diced large |

Bring a very large pot of water to a boil. Use a small, sharp knife to cut the cores out of the cabbages. Boil each cabbage for 10 minutes. Remove and cool under cold running water. Drain. Peel away the large outer leaves until you get to inner cabbage leaves that look too small to stuff. You want to have about 26 large, stuffable leaves. Reserve large outer leaves for stuffing, chop small inner cabbage leaves into chunks.

Mix rice together with onion, carrots, mushrooms, salt, garlic powder, and pepper.

Mix together the ketchup, brown sugar, garlic, salt, and water and set aside.

Place half the cut-up cabbage, together with half the chopped onions, on the bottom of a large, heavy Dutch oven or roasting pan.

Preheat oven to 375°F.

Stuff the large cabbage leaves by placing a spoonful of stuffing in the center of each leaf. Fold over the ribbed end of the leaf, then fold over the two sides and roll up. Place each cabbage roll, fold side down, onto the chopped cabbage and onions in the Dutch oven. When the cabbage leaves are all stuffed and packed into the pot (they will be in one or two layers depending on the pot size), place the rest of the cut-up cabbage and onion over the cabbage rolls. Pour sauce over all, cover tightly, and bake for 45 minutes to 1 hour, until the cabbage is very tender. Serve with noodles and broccoli.

This is delicious served right away, but even better reheated the following day, and the day after.

YIELD: *6 to 8 servings.*

# Stuffed Peppers

4 large or 8 small green bell
    peppers
2 pounds ground chuck or
    round
1 cup cooked rice
1/2 cup matzo meal or bread
    crumbs
1 large onion, minced fine

4 cloves garlic, crushed
1 egg
2 teaspoons salt
1/4 teaspoon freshly ground
    black pepper
2 tablespoons chopped parsley
1/2 cup water
Tomato Sauce (page 170)

Preheat oven to 375°F.

Select peppers that will sit straight. Cut away the stem ends of the peppers, cut out cores, and remove all seeds. If you are using very large peppers, cut them in half lengthwise.

In a large bowl combine ground beef, cooked rice, matzo meal or bread crumbs, minced onion, garlic, egg, salt, pepper, and parsley. Mix well. The best way to do this is with your hands. Add water and mix again.

Stuff the meat mixture into the peppers. Arrange the peppers in a roasting or baking pan just large enough to hold them and pour about 1/2 inch of water into the bottom of the pan. Place a tablespoonful of tomato sauce on each stuffed pepper. Cover with foil and bake for 1 hour and 15 minutes.

Arrange peppers on serving platter and spoon additional tomato sauce over each pepper. Serve with baked or mashed potatoes and a salad.

YIELD: *6 to 8 servings.*

# Vegetarian Stuffed Peppers

6 large green bell peppers
1 large head broccoli, chopped
  small
¼ head cauliflower, chopped
  small
3 carrots, scraped and diced
  small
6 medium mushrooms, diced

1 medium onion, diced small
2 stalks celery, diced small
2 tablespoons corn oil
2 teaspoons salt
¼ teaspoon pepper
2 cups cooked brown rice
2 eggs, beaten

Cut away stem ends from peppers and scoop out seeds and membrane.

Steam broccoli, cauliflower, and carrots until tender. Sauté mushrooms, onions, and celery in corn oil until wilted. Stir in salt and pepper. Mix broccoli, cauliflower, and carrots together with the mushrooms, onions, and celery. Stir in the brown rice. When vegetables are cool, stir in the eggs and mix well.

Preheat oven to 375°F.

Stuff each pepper with the vegetable-rice mixture and place in a baking dish with 1 cup water. Cover with foil and bake for 30 to 40 minutes, or until peppers are tender. Serve with Tomato Sauce (page 170), mashed or baked potatoes, or Mushrooms and Egg Barley (page 92).

YIELD: *6 servings.*

## 10

# SALADS

□ □ □ □ □ □ □ □ □ □ □ □ □ □ □ □ □ □ □ □

I*n a book* called *A Treasury of Jewish Humor,* I found the following passage written by Nathan Ausubel: "For centuries most Jews lived in stony ghettos where no green thing ever showed its natural face. So they became estranged from many vegetables and fruits. Since they were very poor, the principal articles of their diet consisted of herring—the poor Jew's meat—of cheese, potatoes, onions, garlic, dried beans and bread—especially bread. Meat, poultry and fish were usually reserved for the Sabbath and religious festivals."

Salads, the kinds of salads we know today consisting of leafy lettuces, exotic raddichio and arugula, were totally unknown to my mother and grandmother. The closest thing we ate to that kind of salad was coleslaw, and I confess that to this day cabbage is my favorite salad ingredient, and the other salad greens all seem somewhat effete and unsubstantial to me.

The recipe for salads that I know and love best are mostly for what the French call "composed" salads. That is to say, a number of vegetables and other ingredients, such as herring and olives, all organized and held together by a dressing. These salads make a perfectly satisfying meal on their own, so once you have taken the trouble to put them together, you don't really need to make something else "to go with," you can just sit down and enjoy.

## Spring Salad

Too hot to cook? My spring salad makes a really nice lunch or summer-night dinner. The best way to eat this salad is with some good Jewish-style rye bread. If you're on a very strict diet, you can substitute plain low fat yogurt for the sour cream, but it's really not the same. And if you're going to do that, you might as well have melba toast instead of rye bread and be really good. Oh, and make sure you use a low fat cottage cheese.

*2 cups pot cheese or dry cottage cheese*
*1 large cucumber, peeled and diced*
*6 radishes, diced*

*6 cherry tomatoes, quartered*
*2 scallions, chopped crosswise very fine*
*1 cup sour cream*
*Lettuce leaves*

Place pot cheese or cottage cheese in a shallow glass bowl or shape into a mound on a lettuce-lined plate. Arrange diced cucumber on two sides, then place radishes and tomatoes in between. Sprinkle scallions over cheese. Serve sour cream or yogurt in a separate bowl for topping.

YIELD:  *2 servings.*

# Coleslaw

This coleslaw is great as a side dish with cold cuts, hot meat dishes, on sandwiches, at a picinic or a buffet.

*1 large head green cabbage*
*2 large carrots or 4 small*
*1 small red onion*
*1 large green pepper, seeded*
*¼ cup sugar*

*¼ cup white vinegar*
*½ teaspoon freshly ground*
  *black pepper*
*1 cup mayonnaise*

Remove the large outer leaves of the cabbage, cut into quarters, and cut away the inside core. Shred finely, either with a large knife or use the shredding attachment of a food processor. Shred the carrots, onion, and green pepper.

Mix all the shredded vegetables together in a large bowl. In a small bowl whisk sugar and vinegar together until sugar is dissolved. Add pepper and mayonnaise and blend well. Pour over the vegetables and toss together until very well mixed.

YIELD:  *8 to 10 servings.*

# Zippy Coleslaw

This coleslaw is best served freshly made. It may hold for a day or two, but it seems to lose its perky flavor.

*1 large head green cabbage*
*2 large carrots, peeled*
*1 large red onion*
*1 large green pepper, seeded*
*¼ cup sugar*
*¼ cup cider vinegar*

*2 tablespoons Dijon mustard*
*½ teaspoon freshly ground*
  *black pepper*
*¼ teaspoon Tabasco*
*1 cup mayonnaise*

Remove the large outer leaves of the cabbage, cut into quarters, and cut away the inside core. Shred finely, either with a large knife or use the shredding attachment of a food processor. Shred the carrots, onion, and green pepper.

Mix all the shredded vegetables together in a large bowl. In a small bowl whisk sugar and vinegar and mustard together until sugar is dissolved. Add pepper, Tabasco, and mayonnaise and blend well. Pour over the vegetables and toss together until very well mixed.

YIELD: *8 to 10 servings.*

# Cucumber and Onion Salad

If they had anything resembling salads in the old country, this is the kind of salad they ate. You will find versions of this salad all over Russia today when cucumbers are in season.

| | |
|---|---|
| 2 large cucumbers or 4 small | 1/4 cup sugar |
| 2 tablespoons kosher salt | 1/4 cup vinegar |
| 4 cups cold water | 1/4 teaspoon white pepper |
| 1 large onion, thinly sliced | |

Peel and slice the cucumbers very thin. Toss the cucumber slices in a bowl with the salt, add water, and let stand for 30 minutes. Drain and rinse quickly under cold running water.

Place cucumber slices in a bowl with the sliced onion. Combine sugar, vinegar, and white pepper and pour over cucumbers and onions. Mix well. Cover and refrigerate until ready to serve. This salad stays good for 2 to 3 days if refrigerated, but it is best when freshly made.

YIELD: *4 to 6 servings.*

# Greek Salad

When I was a child you could go into one of those marvelous old-fashioned Jewish appetizing stores and indulge your senses in a million ways. You were simply surrounded by wonderful things to eat: hard candies, the kind that had soft jam filling inside, all wrapped in beautiful multicolored papers; barrels of pickles to make your mouth water and pucker; an array of smoked fish that was mind-boggling; and, among the fishes and herrings, potato salads and coleslaw, there was always a beautiful tray of what was called Greek salad. When I grew up I learned that it wasn't really a Greek salad, for obviously herring was substituted for anchovies (a fish not familiar to Eastern European Jews), and there wasn't a trace of feta cheese, so as to keep it parve and kosher, but it was then and still remains one of my all time favorite salads. I've tried to reproduce it to the best of my memory. I hope you like it as much as I do.

Greek salad makes a wonderful summer lunch when served with a hearty black bread and butter and a bowl of cold ruby-red borscht.

4 celery stalks, sliced in 1/2-inch
   pieces
2 cucumbers, peeled and sliced
   into 1/2-inch pieces
2 red onions, quartered and
   sliced
4 tomatoes, cut into eighths
2 carrots, thinly sliced
1 red bell pepper, cored and
   sliced into 1/2-inch pieces

1 green bell pepper, cored and
   sliced into 1/2-inch pieces
Olives, black and green
2 pickled herring fillets, cut into
   small pieces, or a small jar of
   pickled herring tidbits
1/2 cup salad dressing for
   Marinated Mushrooms (page
   36)

In a large bowl combine all the vegetables and the herring and mix well. Add the salad dressing, mix, and let stand for several hours in the refrigerator. Serve with lots of good, hearty bread.

YIELD:   *4 to 6 servings.*

# Health Salad

꒰

This salad can be a vegetarian main dish or a great side dish. I call it a health salad because it has only things that are good for you in it.

*2 cups cooked kidney beans*
*2 cups cooked chick-peas*
*1 pound frozen lima beans*
*2 cups cauliflower, cut into bite-size pieces*
*2 cups broccoli, cut into bite-size pieces*
*2 carrots, scraped and diced*
*¹/₂ cup corn or safflower oil*

*¹/₄ cup wine or cider vinegar*
*¹/₄ cup sugar*
*1 teaspoon dried oregano*
*1 tablespoon kosher salt*
*1 teaspoon freshly ground black pepper*
*1 red pepper, cored and cut into ¹/₂-inch pieces*
*1 large red onion, diced*

In this recipe you can use canned kidney beans and chick-peas. Remove from can and rinse well under running water. If you prefer, soak dry kidney beans and chick-peas (separately) in water to cover overnight. Drain, rinse, and cook (separately) in water to cover, at a low simmer, until tender. The kidney beans will take 1¹/₂ to 2 hours. The chick-peas cook for 2¹/₂ to 3 hours.

Cook frozen lima beans, cauliflower, broccoli, and carrots in water to cover for 3 to 5 minutes and drain.

Combine oil, vinegar, sugar, oregano, salt, and pepper in a large bowl and mix well. Add kidney beans, chick-peas, lima beans, cauliflower, broccoli, carrots, red pepper, and onion, and stir to mix. The salad may be served right away, but it is best if covered and refrigerated overnight. Before serving, drain salad in a large sieve to remove excess dressing. The salad will keep well in the refrigerator for up to 5 days if kept in its dressing.

YIELD:   *8 to 10 servings.*

# Potato Salad

I love potatoes in any shape or form. This potato salad is what I would call the typical, old-fashioned potato salad, in other words, a classic. Enjoy!

| | |
|---|---|
| *2 pounds potatoes, russet or Idaho* | *¼ cup corn oil* |
| *3 scallions, chopped* | *¼ cup cider vinegar* |
| *3 sprigs parsley, chopped* | *½ teaspoon prepared mustard* |
| | *1 cup mayonnaise* |

Peel and cook the potatoes in salted water to cover, until tender but not too soft. Drain and let stand until cool enough to handle. Cut potatoes into cubes and place them in a large mixing bowl. Add the parsley and scallions. Mix oil and vinegar together and pour over the potatoes. Mix well. Mix mustard and mayonnaise together and add to the potatoes when they have cooled completely. Mix well. Serve room temperature or chilled in the refrigerator.

YIELD:   *4 to 6 servings.*

# Russian Potato Salad

This salad is especially delicious if you serve it while the potatoes are still a little warm, but it's still very yummy when cold. Well covered and refrigerated it stays good for 4 to 5 days.

| | |
|---|---|
| *3 pounds small red or new potatoes* | *3 whole scallions, thinly sliced* |
| *½ cup mayonnaise* | *2 teaspoons kosher salt* |
| *½ cup sour cream* | *⅛ teaspoon black pepper* |
| *2 tablespoons fresh dill, finely chopped* | |

Cut potatoes into halves or thirds, depending on their size. Put in a pot with cold water to cover, bring to a boil and cook until they are tender but still firm enough to hold their shape (15 to 20 minutes). Drain the potatoes and place them in a large bowl. Mix together the mayonnaise, sour cream, dill, scallions, salt, and pepper. Add to the potatoes and mix well.

YIELD:  *8 to 12 servings.*

# Three-Bean Salad

2 cups cooked kidney beans
2 cups cooked chick-peas
1 pound frozen lima beans
½ cup corn oil
½ cup wine or cider vinegar
½ cup sugar
1 tablespoon kosher salt
½ teaspoon freshly ground
   black pepper

1 medium red onion, thinly
   sliced
1 small red pepper, cored and
   diced
1 small green pepper, cored and
   diced

You can use canned kidney beans and chick-peas. Remove from the can and rinse well under running water. If you prefer, soak dry kidney beans and chick-peas (separately) in water to cover overnight. Drain, rinse, and cook (separately) in water to cover, at a low simmer, until tender. The kidney beans will take 1½ to 2 hours. The chick-peas cook for 2½ to 3 hours.

Cook lima beans in water to cover for 10 minutes and drain.

Combine oil, vinegar, sugar, salt, and pepper in a large bowl and mix well. Add lima beans, kidney beans, chick-peas, onion, and peppers. Stir to mix, cover, and refrigerate overnight. Before serving, drain the beans in a colander or remove from bowl with a slotted spoon to eliminate excess dressing. This salad will keep well in the refrigerator for up to 7 days if kept in its dressing.

YIELD:  *8 to 10 servings.*

# 11

# VEGETABLES

□ □ □ □ □ □ □ □ □ □ □ □ □ □ □ □ □ □ □ □ □ □ □ □ □ □ □ □ □ □ □ □

**W**hat did my mother and grandmother know of broccoli, asparagus, or spinach in the old country? I think the only green vegetable they knew and trusted was cabbage, and what they did with cabbage was to cook it for a good long time. Later, when they came to America and discovered the convenience of canned goods, they continued cooking in the old way. I remember my mother opening a can of "mixed vegetables," and instead of simply reheating them, she would cook them again to make sure they were "done."

Later on, when we were a little older, my mother learned about the importance of fresh green vegetables from reading a doctor's column in the Jewish newspaper. Green vegetables, it said, were important and beneficial to the growth of healthy children. This she could understand. Then we ate spinach. Remember spinach and Popeye? Well, that was the only way she got me to eat spinach. She never did get the hang of cooking green vegetables. But the root vegetables were a different story—carrots, parsnips, rutabagas, potatoes, onions—these were vegetables she understood and cooked well. These are mostly the vegetables that I've included in this section. Steaming broccoli or asparagus you can do without me.

# Mashed Carrots and Parsnips

Whenever I cooked carrots and parsnips in chicken soup I couldn't help noticing how delicious those two veggies were together—so sweet, tender, and comforting. So I thought, why wait for chicken soup, they can be cooked as a vegetable dish in their own right. A perfect marriage and a great side dish to any meal.

| | |
|---|---|
| *5 to 6 carrots* | *¼ teaspoon white pepper* |
| *4 large or 6 small parsnips* | *3 tablespoons butter or* |
| *2 teaspoons kosher salt* | *margarine* |

Peel the carrots and parsnips and cut into thin (¼ inch) slices. Place in a saucepan with enough cold water to cover by 1 inch. Bring to a boil and reduce to a simmer and cook for 30 to 45 minutes, until vegetables are tender. Drain the carrots and parsnips (you can save the liquid for a soup) and place in the bowl of a food processor. Blend to a puree or use a ricer or potato masher. Stir in salt, pepper, and butter or margarine and serve.

Yield: *6 to 8 servings.*

*Advice from Mama:* Some people might think that 45 minutes is too long to cook carrots and parsnips. I disagree. I happen to like these veggies to be soft, sweet, and almost mushy. If you think you would prefer them less cooked, taste them halfway through and stop cooking them when they are done to your liking. Remember that everyone is an expert in his or her own kitchen.

# Baked Onions

I usually make this dish for our Thanksgiving dinner, and it is a lovely accompaniment with the other side dishes. If you love onions, then serve this dish with any of your favorite entrées.

*2 pounds small white onions*
*2 tablespoons butter or*
  *margarine*
*¼ teaspoon freshly ground*
  *black pepper*

*1 teaspoon kosher salt*
*2 tablespoons sugar*
*¼ cup white vinegar*

Preheat oven to 375°F.

Bring a large pot of water to the boil. Drop in the onions and parboil for 10 minutes. Drain and cool the onions under cold running water. This process makes the onions much easier to peel. Cut away both ends of each onion with a sharp paring knife and peel away the skin. Place the onions in an ovenproof casserole with a cover and add butter or margarine, pepper, salt, sugar, and vinegar. Mix well, cover, and bake in a preheated oven for 45 minutes to 1 hour, until onions are very tender and slightly caramelized. These onions are best served hot or warm.

YIELD: *6 to 8 servings.*

# Baked Beets and Onions

*4 baseball-size yellow onions*
*4 beets, similar size*
*¼ cup corn oil*

*¼ teaspoon freshly ground*
  *black pepper*
*1 teaspoon kosher salt*

Preheat oven to 375°F.

Bring a large pot of water to a boil. Drop in the onions and parboil for 10 minutes. Drain and cool the onions under cold running water. This will make the onions much easier to peel. Cut away both ends of the onions and peel away the skin. Drop the beets in the water and parboil for 10 minutes. Drain and cool the beets under cold running water. Peel the outer skin off the beets. Score the onions and beets with a sharp knife across their tops and bottoms. Place them upright in an ovenproof casserole with a tight-fitting lid. Sprinkle oil, pepper, and salt over the vegetables. Bake for 45 minutes to 1 hour until a sharp knife goes through the vegetables easily. These will taste sweet and savory at the same time.

Y I E L D : *6 to 8 servings.*

## Roasted Garlic Peppers

*¼ cup corn or olive oil*
*2 cloves garlic, crushed*
*¼ teaspoon salt*

*4 red bell peppers*
*2 green bell peppers*

Preheat oven to 375°F. Line a baking sheet with tinfoil.

In a small bowl combine the oil, garlic, and salt and mix together. Cut peppers in half lengthwise, remove core and seeds, and cut into strips about 1 inch wide. Dip each pepper strip into the oil mixture and place, skin side up, on prepared baking sheet. Roast in preheated oven for 20 to 30 minutes, until the edges start to blacken. Serve hot, room temperature, or cold.

Y I E L D : *6 to 8 servings.*

# Mashed Potatoes (Milchig)

I sell lots of mashed potatoes, because people are so happy to find out that mine are "the real thing." But you don't have to wait until you get to Mama Leah's. Here's my recipe. You can make "the real thing" right in your own home and it's so easy. If you have any left over, you can refrigerate them for 4 or 5 days. When you want to reheat, put the mashed potatoes in an ovenproof dish, spread the top with a little butter or margarine, and heat in a 350°F oven for 45 minutes to 1 hour. You'll love the crust that forms on the top. But if you need to reheat quickly, stick them in the microwave.

*6 large russet or Idaho potatoes*  
*2 tablespoons kosher salt*  
*2 tablespoons butter or*  
*margarine*  

*¼ teaspoon white pepper*  
*½ to ¾ cup hot milk*

Peel the potatoes and dice small. Place in a large pot with cold water to cover and add 1 tablespoon salt. Bring to a boil, reduce to a simmer, and cook for 25 to 30 minutes, until fork tender.

Drain the potatoes and place them in a large bowl. Add the remaining salt, butter or margarine, and white pepper. Mash with potato masher or use an electric mixer to whip the potatoes. Gradually add enough hot milk to moisten the puree. Be careful not to overmash or the potatoes will become pasty. Don't worry about a few lumps here and there, just enjoy!

YIELD: *8 to 10 servings.*

# Mashed Potatoes (Flaischig)

My mother kept a semi-kosher home. By that I mean she did not keep separate dishes and pots for meat and dairy meals, but her meat was kosher and she never mixed meat with dairy at a meal. I remember coming home for lunch from public school and getting baby lamb chops and potatoes mashed with grieben. What joy! But what calories!

*6 large russet or Idaho potatoes*
*2 tablespoons kosher salt*
*4 tablespoons margarine or*

*Schmaltz (rendered chicken fat) (see page 10)*
*¼ teaspoon white pepper*

Peel the potatoes and cut into small dice. Place in a large pot with cold water to cover and add 1 tablespoon salt. Bring to a boil, reduce to a simmer, and cook for 25 to 30 minutes, until fork tender.

Drain the potatoes, reserving some of the cooking water, and place potatoes in a large bowl. Add the remaining salt, margarine or schmaltz, and white pepper. Mash with potato masher or use an electric mixer to whip the potatoes. Add a little of the cooking water if necessary to moisten. Be careful not to overmash or the potatoes will become pasty.

YIELD: *6 to 8 servings.*

*Advice from Mama:* A few small lumps here and there are part of the homemade goodness of real mashed potatoes. I guess you could say that mashed potatoes are like life: without an occasional lump, how would you know to enjoy the smooth part?

# Oven Roast Potatoes

My children just love potatoes made this way, especially when they're overcooked. Serve these potatoes with fish, poultry, or beef. A happy vegetarian I know eats them for a meal with a green salad.

*4 large baking potatoes*            *1 teaspoon salt*
*3 tablespoons corn oil*             *1 teaspoon paprika*
*1 teaspoon garlic powder*

Preheat oven to 375°F.

Peel the potatoes, if you wish, but they are delicious roasted with their skins on. Cut the potatoes into large chunks and place in roasting pan. Add the oil and rub it all over the potatoes with your hands, to cover every little bit of exposed potato surface. Mix together garlic powder, salt, and paprika and sprinkle on the potatoes and mix. Bake for 30 minutes, toss potatoes with a spatula and bake another 30 minutes. If you bake a little longer, that won't hurt them. I once forgot they were in the oven and baked them for 2 hours. They were still crispy, crunchy, and delicious. Serve hot or warm. These potatoes are always a hit.

YIELD:  *4 to 6 servings.*

# Mashed Rutabaga

I always serve this at Thanksgiving as one of the vegetables, along with baked onions, candied sweet potatoes, mashed potatoes, and a green vegetable.

*1 large rutabaga*                   *¹/₄ teaspoon white pepper*
*3 quarts salted water*              *¹/₄ pound butter or margarine*
*1 tablespoon kosher salt*

Peel the rutabaga and slice as thin as possible. Boil in salted water for 1 hour or until tender. Drain and place in food processor with salt, pepper, and butter or margarine. Process to a puree.

Y I E L D :   *6 to 8 servings.*

## Acorn Squash

This is another one of those dishes that seem to go so well with roast turkey, especially at Thanksgiving. However, my family loves it anytime.

*2 large acorn squash*
*2 teaspoons salt*
*3 tablespoons brown sugar*
*4 tablespoons butter or*
  *margarine*

*1 tablespoon brown sugar*
*½ teaspoon cinnamon*

Wash and quarter the squash and scoop out the seeds. Place in a pot with enough water to just cover. Bring to a boil, reduce to a simmer, and cook for 30 to 45 minutes, until the squash is tender. Remove from heat, drain, and let cool.

Preheat oven to 375°F.

When the squash is cool enough to handle, scoop out the pulp and discard the skin. Place the pulp in a bowl and add the salt, sugar, and 3 tablespoons of butter or margarine. Mash with a fork and blend well or beat with an electric mixer. Place in a buttered casserole. Mix together the sugar and cinnamon and sprinkle over the top. Dot with remaining tablespoon of butter or margarine. Bake in preheated oven for 10 to 15 minutes, or until the top browns slightly.

Y I E L D :   *6 to 8 servings.*

# Candied Sweet Potatoes

I think of this dish as typically American, always a favorite with turkey, but it is one that every ethnic group would love.

*6 to 8 sweet potatoes or yams*  
*½ cup brown sugar*  
*¼ cup maple syrup*  
*1 teaspoon cinnamon*

*8 whole cloves*  
*¾ cup water*  
*3 tablespoons butter or*  
  *margarine*

Preheat oven to 375°F.

Peel the sweet potatoes or yams and cut in half lengthwise. Place in a buttered or oiled baking dish. In a saucepan combine brown sugar, maple syrup, cinnamon, cloves, water, and butter or margarine. Cook over moderate heat, stirring, until the sugar has completely dissolved. Pour this mixture over the sweet potatoes and bake uncovered in a preheated oven for about 1 hour, until soft and glazed.

YIELD:   *8 to 12 servings.*

# Tzimmes (Parve)

I make this tzimmes twice a year, for Rosh Hashana and Passover, to mark the symbolism of a sweet holiday. My mother never cooked this at home because she didn't care for it. As a result I never tasted it until I personally experimented making it because of customers' requests. I love it now and don't know why my mother didn't.

*10 to 12 large carrots, peeled*  
  *and cut into large chunks*

*2 medium russet or Idaho*  
  *potatoes, peeled and cubed*

3 yams or sweet potatoes, peeled
   and cubed
1 medium onion, diced
10 large pitted prunes, cut in
   half

1 clove garlic, crushed
½ cup brown sugar
1 teaspoon salt
1 teaspoon cinnamon (optional)
2 cups orange juice

Place all the ingredients in a large saucepan and bring to a boil. Immediately reduce the heat to a simmer and cook over low heat, stirring often, for approximately 1 hour. If the tzimmes starts to get dry, add ½ cup of water at a time. Cook until the carrots are very soft, but not mushy. The consistency should be moist and thick.

YIELD:    *8 to 12 servings.*

# 12

# PASSOVER

□ □ □ □ □ □ □ □ □ □ □ □ □ □ □ □ □ □ □ □ □ □ □ □ □ □ □ □

T*he Passover season* is a wonderful time for Jews all over the world, and the most important part of it, of course, is the ritual meal called a Seder. This celebration is particularly special to me because at its very core it is concerned with food. The roots of the holiday go way back to primitive times when people made sacrifices each spring to ensure a prosperous year. Herdsmen would sacrifice a sheep, maybe or a goat; farmers—maybe they sacrificed some grain. These are traditions that got started many, many centuries before the Exodus out of Egypt. Now, if you ask me what Jewish holidays are all about, I'll tell you this: they are about warmth and friends and family and sharing and about tradition. That's what all of them are about, but this one, this holiday in particular, is about remembering the trials of the people of Israel, and about their deliverance from slavery. That's the story that's told in the Haggadah, the book that's read at every Seder, and it's behind the special ritual foods that are eaten at the Seder, too.

No question about it, the most important item on the Passover table is the matzo, unleavened bread, flat as a pancake, crisp as a cracker, and square like a . . . well . . . like a square. All year long we eat every kind of bread. We've got bagels, and challah, and rye bread (maybe with seeds, maybe without) you could die for, but on Passover we eat only matzos because when our people fled from Pharaoh, no one had time to wait around for bread to rise.

We're talking here symbols. On the Seder table is always a special plate, and on it symbolic food. First of all there's the *ze'ro'a,* that's a roasted bone, and *bay'tza,* that's a roasted egg, both symbolic of a very ancient tradition of springtime sacrifices. Moses told his people that everyone had to mark his door with the blood of the lamb. Why? So that the Angel of Death, who was coming to punish the Egyptian oppressors, would know who was who, and what was what, and he would pass over their homes. That's why the holiday is called "Passover." The root of the word "Paschal" means "pass over" in Hebrew. Then there is *maror,* that's bitter herbs (usually horseradish), and it symbolizes the bitterness of the plight of the people, and there's saltwater, which helps us remember their tears. And there's also sweet *haroset,* which is nuts and fruits and spices all chopped up together and mixed with wine to stand for the mortar with which they were forced to build all those pyramids in Egypt, and, finally, the *karpas,* fresh greens like parsley or celery, to symbolize the season of spring.

So Passover is meant to bring back bitter memories, but mostly it's meant to remind us how good we have it now. It's really a holiday of redemption, and everyone is supposed to be in a very jolly mood—which they mostly are, especially once the service is over and everyone can finally get something nonsymbolic to eat. For the children it is always a very special time because they are usually allowed to sip a little wine in the course of the service, and they get to steal a special piece of matzo called the *afikomen.* Later, when the grown-ups are full and usually feeling very mellow, the *kinder* (children) will extort a gift for its return.

I remember the Seders of my childhood with great fondness, probably in part because my poor father could never, never get through the entire service. The Haggadah—let's be honest—is very long and a little boring to small children, and, to tell you the truth,

we weren't the best-behaved children in all of God's creation, especially after a little Manischewitz wine had found its way past our
lips. In fact, I remember one Seder when my sister Shirley became
so tipsy that she threw a wishbone at my father while he was
reading from the holy book, shouting, "Catch, Papa!" My sister
Libby and my cousin Mildred didn't know whether to gasp with
horror or to burst out laughing—I think we did both. And then my
father, who rarely ever became angry with us, pounded his fist on
the table for order and swore a great oath that he would never
conduct another Seder with us in attendance. Come to think of it,
it was an oath he uttered yearly and one I'm glad to say he never
kept.

Maybe the best Seders of all, though, were the ones my husband,
Stanley, conducted at our restaurant. We would invite all our close
friends and relatives and sometimes we had a professional singer
come, and then everyone would join in singing the traditional
Seder songs that we all remembered, and the wonderful Yiddish
songs that only the grown-ups seemed to know. Stanley is gone
now, but my son, Bennett, conducts our Seders with great pride
and panache.

## Special Passover Foods

During the eight days of Passover, certain foods have come to be
traditional. The most important restriction to observe is that of not
using any type of flour that might ferment and rise. The only flour
used during Passover is made from the traditional Passover matzo
and is called matzo cake meal. The only other ingredient used in
baking or thickening is potato starch.

Obviously the most important meal of Passover is the Seder,
which is held on the first and second nights. In my family the
traditional Seder dinner included various combinations of the following dishes. A lot depended on how many people were coming
to dinner. If we had a huge party, we might have all of the appetizers, two or three entrées, and several side dishes.

For appetizers we always have Gefilte Fish or Chopped Chicken Liver or melon, or all three. Then there is always Chicken Soup with Matzo Balls. For the main course there might be Brisket in Natural Gravy, Pot Roast, Stuffed Breast of Veal, Roast Lemon-Garlic Chicken or Poached Salmon with Cucumber-Dill Sauce. Side dishes always included a Potato Kugel, Passover Knishes, and Tzimmes. For dessert there might be Passover Honey Cake, Sponge Cake, and Macaroons with fresh fruit.

Other traditional Passover foods that you will find in other parts of the book are: Chopped Calf's Liver, Roast Stuffed Derma, Cold Beet Borscht, Plain Roast Chicken, Fricassee of Chicken Giblets, Potted Breast of Veal, Glazed Brisket, and Polish-Jewish Pot Roast.

## Gefilte Fish

There is an old Jewish saying that goes, "Without fish there is no Sabbath," and, sure enough, every Friday afternoon, when I came home from school, the smell of cooking gefilte fish assaulted my nostrils as soon as I stepped into the lobby of our apartment building. I hated the smell and I wasn't crazy about the gefilte fish, either. I would eat a little if it was served cold, but wouldn't touch it warm. Needless to say, as I grew to adulthood, my appreciation for this delicacy grew, too. I used to add pike and a little carp to the mix of fish, but when I heard that pike and carp were full of PCBs, I started to just use whitefish and thought it made a more delicate and sweeter gefilte fish.

Incidentally, if you've ever wondered why gefilte fish is so inextricably associated with the Sabbath, the answer lies in the Talmud. It seems that separating the flesh of a fish from its bones before eating was considered work, and work is, of course, prohibited on the Sabbath. Never mind the poor housewife who had to work twice as hard in order to be able to relax.

### For the Fish Stock

*Heads and bones from 2 pounds
  of fish such as whitefish, pike,
  or carp, or any other firm,
  white-fleshed, freshwater fish*
*10 cups water*
*1 onion, quartered*

*1 carrot, cut into chunks*
*1 stalk celery*
*Several sprigs parsley*
*1 tablespoon salt*
*½ teaspoon white pepper*

### For the Gefilte Fish

*2 pounds boneless, skinless fillets
  of whitefish, pike, or carp, or
  any other firm, white-fleshed,
  freshwater fish*
*2 medium or 1 very large
  Bermuda onion*
*3 eggs*

*1 teaspoon kosher salt*
*¼ teaspoon white pepper*
*¼ to ½ cup matzo meal*
*1 carrot, peeled and thinly sliced
  (optional)*
*Parsley sprigs, for garnish*

Put the fish head and bones in a large pot, together with the water, onion, carrot, celery, parsley, salt, and pepper. The water should just cover the fish, so add more if necessary. Bring to a boil, lower heat, and simmer for about 30 minutes. In the meantime, prepare the gefilte fish.

Wash fish fillets carefully to remove any scales. Grind fish and onions together. Add eggs, salt, and pepper and mix well. Gradually blend in enough matzo meal to just bind the mixture. The right consistency should be that of a hamburger, not too firm, not too soft. Cover the mixture and refrigerate.

Strain the fish stock to remove all the vegetables and trimmings. Pour the clear fish broth into a clean kettle. Add the sliced carrot if you are using it and taste for seasonings. Add salt and white pepper if necessary. Simmer gently over low heat while you form the gefilte fish.

Wet your hands in cold water and shape the fish mixture into egg-size ovals (they will expand as they cook). Use a long-handled spoon to lower them into simmering stock. Cover and simmer over very low heat for 1 hour.

Let the gefilte fish cool in the stock until it is at room temperature. Remove to serving bowl, garnish with carrot slices and parsley, and pour fish stock over all. Cover and refrigerate overnight or for several hours until the stock has jelled.

Serve with red horseradish.

YIELD: *10 to 12 gefilte fish pieces.*

# Matzo Balls (Knaidlach)
### ▼

My mother made matzo balls in her usual *schit arein* (a little bit of this, a little bit of that) kind of way. Sometimes they came out light and fluffy, other times they would sink to the bottom of the pot and stay there. Now, the ones that floated were delicious and melted in your mouth. But the ones that sank had a nice chewy quality to them that was delicious, too. The ones in my recipe should come out light and fluffy, which is the way I usually prefer them, but once in a while I wish I knew how to make the dense, chewy kind. Any ideas?

| | |
|---|---|
| *4 eggs* | *1 teaspoon salt* |
| *4 tablespoons corn oil* | *¼ teaspoon white pepper* |
| *4 tablespoons cold water or cold* | *½ cup matzo meal* |
| *chicken soup* | *Small bowl of ice water* |

In a bowl beat together the eggs and corn oil. Beat in the water or chicken soup, salt, and white pepper. Gradually add the matzo meal and blend thoroughly. Cover and refrigerate for 30 to 45 minutes.

Bring a large pot of salted water to a boil. Take a teaspoonful or tablespoonful of matzo meal mix (depending on the size matzo balls you like), dip your hands in ice water and quickly roll the mixture into a ball. Drop matzo balls gently into boiling water. Lower the heat to a simmer, cover, and cook for 45 minutes. Test one matzo ball for doneness by cutting it in half to see if it is cooked through all the way to the center. If it is not done, the center will look darker and raw. Cook 10 minutes longer if not done. Remove with slotted spoon and serve in bowls of Chicken Soup (page 64).

YIELD: *15 to 20 matzo balls.*

*Advice from Mama:* You can freeze matzo balls very successfully. Place them in a plastic container and fill with cooking water or chicken soup to cover. Cover the container tightly and freeze.

# Mandlen (Soup Nuts)

Mandlen, which means "soup nuts," are used as a garnish for soup, usually during Passover because matzo cake meal is used instead of flour. Even the most delicious matzo balls can become boring if you have them for all the eight days of Passover, so mandlen make a nice change in taste and texture.

| | |
|---|---|
| *4 eggs* | *¹/₂ cup matzo cake meal* |
| *1¹/₂ teaspoons salt* | *¹/₄ cup potato starch* |
| *Pinch of white pepper* | *¹/₂ to 1 cup corn oil* |

In a bowl beat together the eggs and salt. Gradually beat in the matzo cake meal and potato starch and beat until well blended. Heat the oil in a skillet. When it is very hot, drop batter by teaspoonfuls and fry until crispy brown on each side. Drain on paper towels and serve in soup.

YIELD: *24 to 30 mandlen.*

*Advice from Mama:* The mandlen I make are never perfectly round and even in size, but that is part of their homemade charm. If you want even, get store-bought.

# Potato Knaidlach (Dumplings)

When you think of things to put into the soup and you want to go beyond matzo balls, potato dumplings make a great change. But going beyond soup, some people like to serve these dumplings with pot roast or brisket. That's good, too.

| | |
|---|---|
| *3 or 4 large potatoes, peeled and quartered* | *½ small onion, finely minced* |
| *4 teaspoons salt* | *3 eggs, beaten* |
| *2 tablespoons corn oil* | *¼ teaspoon white pepper* |
| | *1 cup matzo meal* |

Place the potatoes in a saucepan with cold water to cover and add 2 teaspoons salt. Bring to a boil, reduce to a simmer, and cook until tender, 25 to 30 minutes. In the meantime heat the oil in a skillet and sauté the onion until golden. Drain the onion and discard the oil.

When potatoes are fork tender, drain them, put them in a bowl, and mash them. Let cool and mix together with onion, eggs, remaining 2 teaspoons salt, pepper, and matzo meal. Knead this mixture until smooth and well blended. Take 1 tablespoon at a time and roll into balls.

Set a large quantity of lightly salted water to boil. Drop the knaidlach into boiling water and cook at a gentle simmer for 20 minutes. Remove with slotted spoon and serve with a roast chicken, pot roast, or your favorite entrée as a substitute for noodles or baked potatoes.

YIELD: *12 to 16 dumplings.*

*Advice from Mama:*

1. Even if you're tempted to make a shortcut and cook the dumplings in the soup, don't. It will make your soup look cloudy and the taste of the soup changes as well.
2. You can add a little chopped fresh dill or parsley or both to the potato mixture.

# Matzo Brei

My son, Bennett, thinks that the second best thing about Passover (our Seder being the first), is my matzo brei.

Matzo brei on Sunday mornings is one of the great pleasures of this life. It gives you strength to read the paper and a good reason to go for a nice long walk afterward. Matzo brei cooks fall into two distinct camps—those who cook it like a pancake, all in one piece, and those who scramble the matzo brei, like scrambled eggs. Both ways are delicious, and you'll just have to decide for yourself which way makes you happier.

| | |
|---|---|
| *8 eggs* | *8 matzos* |
| *½ cup milk* | *Butter or margarine for frying* |
| *1 teaspoon salt* | |

Beat the eggs together with the milk and salt. Run hot water over matzos on each side for a few seconds. Break matzos into pieces and soak in egg mixture. Let stand 10 to 15 minutes. Heat 2 to 3 tablespoons butter or margarine in a large, heavy frying pan and pour in matzo mixture. Cook over medium heat until eggs have set to your liking, preferably golden brown like French toast. If you like your matzo brei cooked pancake-style, turn the matzo brei over, using two large spatulas, and sauté until browned. If you like it scrambled, treat it just like scrambled eggs, but cook until it is browned and crisp. The pancake should be cut into quarters and the scrambled matzo brei divided into 4 portions.

Serve with sugar, jam, or syrup. I personally like it plain or with a little salt sprinkled on before eating.

Y I E L D :   *4 servings.*

# Matzo Brei with Onion

Another version of this recipe was once given to me by a very elderly lady and it was delicious but much more time-consuming to make. She carefully broke each matzo into thirds and softened them slightly in hot water. Then she dipped the matzo pieces first into the egg mixture, then into the sautéed onions, which had been drained of excess oil. The she sautéed the matzos in butter until they were crisp on both sides. My recipe is much more simple but still very delicious.

| | |
|---|---|
| *8 eggs* | *4 tablespoons butter or* |
| *½ cup milk* | *   margarine* |
| *1 teaspoon salt* | *1 large onion, finely diced* |
| *8 matzos* | |

Beat the eggs together with the milk and salt. Run hot water over matzos on each side for a few seconds. Break matzos into pieces and soak in egg mixture. Let stand 10 to 15 minutes. Heat the butter or margarine in a large frying pan. Sauté the onion until it is golden brown. Pour in matzo mixture and stir to mix well. Cook over medium heat until eggs have set to your liking, preferably golden brown like French toast. If you like your matzo brei cooked pancake-style, turn the matzo brei over, using two large spatulas, and sauté until browned. If you like it scrambled, treat it just like scrambled eggs but cook until it is browned and crisp. The pancake should be cut into quarters and the scrambled matzo brei divided into 4 portions. For a very hearty breakfast or brunch, serve with a couple of slices of smoked salmon.

YIELD: *4 servings.*

# Matzo Meal Onion Kugel

2 medium onions, diced fine
1/4 cup corn oil or Schmaltz
    (rendered chicken fat) (page
    10)
8 egg yolks

1/2 cup matzo meal
2 teaspoons salt
1/2 teaspoon white pepper
8 egg whites, at room
    temperature

Preheat oven to 350°F.

Sauté the onions in corn oil until they are lightly browned. Remove from heat and let cool. Beat the egg yolks in a mixer until they thicken slightly and become light and fluffy. Fold sautéed onions, matzo meal, salt, and pepper into the egg yolks. In another bowl beat the egg whites until they start to form stiff peaks and fold them into egg yolk mixture. Grease a 2-quart casserole or soufflé dish and pour in the mixture. Bake for 45 minutes to 1 hour, or until the kugel is set and golden brown on top.

Serve as a side dish with either meat or poultry.

YIELD:  *10 to 14 pieces.*

# Esther's Passover Knishes

I don't know of anybody who made knishes this way, because usually knishes are made with a dough covering, but because you can't use flour at Passover, my mother made these knishes her own special way. What I don't know is the derivation of the recipe. I never asked her when she was alive, where this recipe came from. . . . And, of course, I'm sorry now, all these years later. But everyone, all the cousins, the aunts, the uncles, everyone, acknowledged that my mother, Esther, made the best knishes. And you know what, delicious as they are, they're very easy to make. Much easier, and much quicker, than dough-covered knishes. I learned from watching my mother make them and this, too, is a kind of *schit arein* (a little bit of this, a little bit of that) recipe. If you put in a little too much cake meal, or two extra eggs, or a little extra chicken fat, it doesn't matter. It'll still be delicious. The only thing you have to really pay attention to is to make sure the potato mixture is not too loose. You should be able to handle it. But if you find it's too mushy, just add a little more cake meal until it holds together.

My mother served these knishes not just at Passover, but for any holiday or special occasion. Serve them like you would ordinary potatoes with any meat or chicken, and, remember, they make a great nosh all by themselves.

*2 large onions, diced*

*1½ cups Schmaltz (rendered chicken fat) (page 10)*

*6 large Idaho or russet potatoes (about 5 pounds), peeled and sliced*

*2 tablespoons salt*

*4 eggs*

*2 cups matzo cake meal*

*1 cup chopped liver (recipe follows)*

## Chopped Liver Filling

*½ pound calf's liver*

*3 tablespoons rendered chicken fat with grieben and onions*

*1 teaspoon salt or to taste*

Sauté the onions in the schmaltz until they are nice and brown. Remove 3 tablespoons and set aside for the chopped liver filling. Strain the fat while it is still warm and liquid, to remove the onions and little pieces of grieben, if any. Save the browned onions and grieben.

Broil liver for 5 minutes on each side, until well cooked. It should be very well done, showing no blood at all. Put the well-cooked liver through a meat grinder together with 3 tablespoons of schmaltz or use a food processor. Be careful not to overprocess to a fine puree. Add salt to taste and set aside.

Cook the potatoes in salted water to cover, until they are very tender. Drain and reserve. Measure out ½ cup of the schmaltz and mix together with reserved sautéed onions and grieben. Mix together with the cooked potatoes. Add salt and if potato mixture is cool enough, add the eggs. Beat with an electric mixer. Add matzo cake meal and mix well. It is fine for the potato mixture to be somewhat lumpy.

*To make the knishes:* Place a large tablespoonful of the potato dough on the palm of your hand and flatten into a circle a little bigger than your palm and about ½ inch thick. It helps to keep your hands dusted with matzo cake meal while you work. Place a large teaspoonful of the chopped liver in the center and bring the edges of the potato dough over to enclose the liver. Press gently into an oval or round-shaped knish. Place the formed knishes on a large pan or platter that has been liberally sprinkled with matzo cake meal. Sprinkle a little more matzo cake meal over the knishes. Repeat, until all the knishes are made.

At this point the knishes can be cooked immediately, or covered and refrigerated for a day or two before frying.

*To fry the knishes:* Place about ¼ cup of the rendered chicken fat in a frying pan. Sauté the knishes in hot fat on both sides until golden brown. Add more chicken fat as needed. Keep the knishes warm in a 250°F oven until ready to serve.

YIELD: *Approximately 20 pieces.*

*Advice from Mama:*

1. Knishes can be made without liver filling. Just take a large spoonful of potatoes and pat into a round or oval shape. Proceed as described above.
2. The chopped liver filling can be made a day or two in advance.
3. If you prefer, you can sauté the knishes in oil instead of schmaltz, but you cannot substitute oil for the schmaltz in the knishes, as the taste will be completely wrong.
4. You can fry the knishes hours before serving. Reheat them in a 375°F oven for 15 to 20 minutes.

# Matzo Latkes

Matzo latkes are pancakes made with matzo meal instead of flour—is there anything else to say about them? Yes. They are delicious and perfect for Passover.

4 egg yolks
3/4 cup milk or water
1 cup matzo meal
1 tablespoon sugar
1 teaspoon salt

4 egg whites, at room
  temperature
2 to 4 tablespoons butter or
  margarine for frying

Beat the egg yolks until they are light and frothy. Stir in milk or water, matzo meal, sugar, and salt. Beat the egg whites until they form stiff peaks and fold them into egg-matzo mixture. Melt some butter or margarine in a frying pan. When hot, drop in matzo mixture a tablespoonful at a time. Fry until brown on each side. Repeat until all are done.

Serve for breakfast with jam or syrup.

YIELD: *4 to 6 servings.*

*Advice from Mama:* If you would like these pancakes as an accompaniment to a meat meal, eliminate the sugar and add 1/4 teaspoon white pepper.

# Matzo Cheese Latkes

4 egg yolks
8 ounces pot cheese or cottage
  cheese, well drained
1 1/2 cups matzo meal
2 to 3 tablespoons sugar
1/2 teaspoon cinnamon

Salt to taste
4 egg whites, at room
  temperature
3 to 4 tablespoons butter or
  margarine for frying

Beat the egg yolks until they are light and fluffy, then stir in cheese, matzo meal, sugar, and cinnamon. Mix well. Taste and add salt if necessary. Beat the egg whites until they form stiff peaks and fold into cheese-matzo batter.

Melt some butter or margarine in a nonstick frying pan. Drop batter by heaping tablespoonfuls into hot butter or margarine and fry until golden brown on both sides. Continue until all are done.

Serve with sour cream, your favorite syrup, or jam.

YIELD: *4 to 6 servings.*

# Matzo Chremslach

This makes a lovely brunch or dessert dish anytime, but particularly during Passover.

*6 matzos*　　　　　　　　　　*½ cup sugar*
*6 egg yolks*　　　　　　　　　*½ teaspoon salt*
*Juice of 1 lemon*　　　　　　　*6 egg whites, at room*
*¼ cup raisins*　　　　　　　　　　*temperature*
*¼ cup chopped walnuts or*　　　*Butter or margarine for frying*
　*pecans*

Break the matzos into small pieces and put them in a bowl. Pour boiling water over the matzos to just cover. Set aside for 10 or 15 minutes. When the water has cooled and the matzos are soft, pour off the water and squeeze the matzos with your hands to remove excess moisture. Place the matzos in a bowl and add egg yolks, lemon juice, raisins, nuts, sugar, and salt. Mix well.

In a separate bowl, beat the egg whites until stiff and fold them into the matzo mixture. Heat about 2 tablespoons of butter or margarine in a heavy frying pan and drop spoonfuls of matzo mixture into the hot butter. Fry until golden brown on both sides.

Remove to a platter lined with paper towels. Repeat until all are done.

Serve with strawberry or blueberry syrup.

YIELD:  *4 servings.*

# Haroset (Ashkenazi)

Haroset is made only at Passover and served during the Seder. It symbolizes the mortar that the Jewish slaves were forced to use to build the Pharaoh's monuments. It may symbolize affliction, but it's so good that it's no hardship to eat it. As a result, you have to make lots to make sure there's enough to go around. This haroset can be made several days in advance and be kept covered in the refrigerator.

*4 large apples, peeled, cored,
   and finely chopped
1 teaspoon lemon juice
1 cup walnuts, finely chopped*

*4 tablespoons brown sugar or
   honey
1 teaspoon cinnamon
1/3 cup sweet Passover wine*

In a mixing bowl toss apples with lemon juice. Add the walnuts, sugar or honey, cinnamon, and wine and mix well. Place some on the Seder plate and the rest in a bowl to be served at the Seder table.

YIELD:  *Approximately 4 cups.*

# Haroset (Sephardic)

Sephardic haroset is always made with dried fruits because they were readily available to the Middle Eastern and Spanish-Portuguese Jews.

*Juice of 1 lemon*
*3 large apples, peeled, cored,*
    *and sliced*
*1 cup pitted dates*

*1 cup dried apricots*
*½ cup raisins*
*¼ cup sweet Passover wine*
*½ cup chopped walnuts*

Sprinkle the lemon juice over the sliced apples and set aside. Combine dates, apricots, and raisins in a small saucepan and add just enough water to cover. Bring to a boil, reduce heat to a simmer, and cook until all the fruits are soft, about 20 minutes. Remove from heat, drain, and cool.

Place cooled dates, apricots, and raisins in the bowl of a food processor. Add apple slices and wine and process to a coarse consistency. Remove and mix with walnuts. If you prefer a more uniform consistency, add walnuts to food processor along with other ingredients and process together.

Serve in a bowl or chill the haroset and roll into walnut-size balls.

YIELD:  *Approximately 4 cups.*

# Prune-Nut Squares

———————— ❣ ————————

This makes a great Passover dessert because it doesn't need any flour.

*1 cup pitted prunes*
*4 eggs*
*¹/₂ cup sugar (less, if you like)*

*1 cup chopped walnuts or*
*    pecans*
*1 orange*

Soak prunes in water to cover overnight. Drain and cut into quarters.

Preheat oven to 350°F. Oil an 8-by-8-inch (or 6-by-10-inch) baking pan.

Quarter the orange, remove seeds, and grind it together with the peel in a food processor or electric grinder.

Beat eggs and sugar together until thick. Mix together with prunes, walnuts or pecans, and ground orange and juices. Spread mixture evenly in prepared baking pan and bake 30 minutes in preheated oven. Remove and let cool in pan. When cool, cut into 2-inch squares.

YIELD:  *8 squares.*

# Coconut Macaroons

———————— ❣ ————————

*8 egg whites, at room*
*    temperature*
*1¹/₃ cups sugar*
*¹/₄ teaspoon salt*

*¹/₂ teaspoon vanilla*
*2¹/₂ cups moist shredded*
*    coconut*

Preheat oven to 325°F. Line a baking sheet with baking parchment paper.

Beat the egg whites until they form stiff peaks. Gradually beat in the sugar, salt, and vanilla. Fold in the shredded coconut. Drop the mixture by rounded teaspoonfuls on prepared baking sheet, leaving a 2-inch space between each macaroon.

Bake in preheated oven for 20 to 30 minutes, until macaroons are very lightly browned. Let cool on baking sheet until macaroons are firm.

YIELD:  *35 to 45 macaroons.*

# Baked Fruit Compote for Passover

Macaroons are a typical Passover dessert, and since homemade ones dry out within a few days, this dessert helps use up the leftovers.

*2 pounds mixed dried fruits
    (prunes, apricots, pineapple,
    pears, and figs)*
*¹/₂ cup orange juice*
*¹/₂ cup water*
*6 cloves*

*1 stick cinnamon (or ¹/₂
    teaspoon powdered cinnamon)*
*1 tablespoon lemon juice*
*¹/₂ cup sugar*
*8 to 10 macaroons, crumbled*

Soak dried fruits in cold water to cover overnight. Drain the fruit and place in a saucepan together with the orange juice, water, cloves, and cinnamon. Simmer gently for 45 minutes, then add lemon juice and sugar and cook, stirring frequently, for 10 minutes longer.

Preheat oven to 375°F.

Drain the fruit, reserving the liquid, and place fruit in a shallow ovenproof casserole or pie plate. Add just enough liquid to barely cover the fruit. Sprinkle crumbled macaroons over the top. Bake in preheated oven for 15 to 20 minutes. Serve either warm or cold.

YIELD:  *8 to 10 servings.*

# Chocolate Almond Macaroons

*8 egg whites, at room
  temperature*
*²/₃ cup cocoa*
*²/₃ cup confectioners' sugar*

*¹/₄ teaspoon salt*
*¹/₂ teaspoon vanilla extract*
*1 ¹/₃ cups (8 ounces) chopped
  almonds*

Preheat oven to 325°F. Line a baking sheet with parchment paper.

Beat the egg whites until they form stiff peaks. Gradually beat in the cocoa, confectioner's sugar, salt, and vanilla. Gently fold in the ground almonds. Drop the mixture by rounded teaspoonfuls on prepared baking sheet, leaving a 2-inch space between each macaroon.

Bake in preheated oven for 20 to 30 minutes, until macaroons are very lightly browned. Let cool on baking sheet until macaroons are firm.

YIELD: *35 to 45 macaroons.*

# Passover Honey Cake

At a recent Seder I told my friend Ruth Imber that I had made a quantity of Passover honey cake but I was nervous that it might have come out a little heavy. Ruth, bless her heart, said, "Leah, I don't care how heavy your honey cake came out, it couldn't hold a candle to my Aunt Essie's. When she made honey cake, we all made sure we had an appointment at the dentist the next day."

1 orange
1 cup brown sugar
8 eggs yolks
1 16-ounce jar of honey
1½ cups potato starch
1 cup matzo cake meal
½ teaspoon cinnamon
½ teaspoon cloves

½ teaspoon salt
¾ cup black coffee
1 cup pitted prunes, cut in half
½ cup raisins
½ cup walnuts or pecans,
    chopped
8 egg whites

Quarter the orange, remove any visible seeds, and grind it together with the peel in a food processor or electric grinder.

In a bowl beat together the sugar and egg yolks until very light and frothy. Add honey and ground orange and mix well. In a separate bowl mix together 1¼ cups potato starch, matzo cake meal, cinnamon, cloves, and salt. Gradually beat the dry ingredients into the honey mixture alternately with the black coffee until well blended.

Preheat oven to 350°F. Grease the insides of two 9-by-5-by-3-inch loaf pans with oil and line the bottom with parchment paper.

Mix the remaining ¼ cup potato starch together with the prunes, raisins, and nuts, making sure that everything gets a nice coating of the starch. This will prevent the fruit and nuts from sinking to the bottom of the cake. Fold gently into the cake batter. Beat the egg whites until they are stiff and form peaks and fold egg whites into the cake batter. Spoon the batter into the prepared pans. Bake for approximately 1 hour. To test if the cake is done, insert a toothpick into the center. If it comes out clean, the cake is done. If still moist, bake for an additional 15 minutes.

YIELD:  *2 Passover honey cakes.*

# Passover Orange Sponge Cake

*1 orange*
*10 eggs, separated*
*1 cup sugar*

*½ cup matzo cake meal*
*¼ cup potato starch*

Preheat oven to 350°F.

Quarter the orange, remove any visible seeds, and grind it together with the peel in a food processor or electric grinder.

Beat together egg yolks and sugar until light and fluffy. Beat in ground orange and juice and gradually beat in matzo cake meal and potato starch. Beat the egg whites until they form stiff peaks and fold into the cake batter. Pour cake batter into an ungreased 9-inch tube pan and bake in preheated oven for 1 hour. Test with a toothpick for doneness. Remove from oven and invert tube pan onto a large plate. Let stand until cool, then shake out sponge cake.

YIELD:   *One 9-inch sponge cake.*

# 13

# BREADS *and*
# BAGELS

□ □ □ □ □ □ □ □ □ □ □ □ □ □ □ □ □ □ □ □ □ □ □ □ □ □ □ □ □ □ □

**W***hy should you bake* your own breads and bagels when
you can buy perfectly good ones from the store?

Well, first of all, you may live in a place where the stores sell
nothing more exotic than Wonder Bread, in which case, if you
want good bread, you have no choice but to bake your own. But
even if you're surrounded by great bakeries on every corner, I still
think you should occasionally bake your own bread. For one
thing, you get a wonderful feeling of accomplishment that no
other kind of cooking can give you. For another thing, by baking
your own bread you get a little exercise when you knead the dough
so that later, when you eat the bread, you don't have to feel guilty
about all those calories. And, finally, nothing in the whole wide
world smells as good as bread baking in the oven. Great writers
and poets have filled their works with nostalgic descriptions of the
aromas of their mother's home-baked breads. If you want your
children to have fond memories of you and your cooking when

they grow up, the best way to insure that is to bake your own bread.

If you have ever eaten any of these breads, rolls, or bagels, freshly baked out of a home oven, then you know how delicious they are. If you haven't, then roll up your sleeves and get to work because the end result will be worth the trouble. And you know what? Baking your own bread is not even all that much trouble. You get to do a little bit of work and the yeast and your oven do all the rest.

My mouth waters even now when I think of a freshly baked, still warm, onion pletzel lathered with sweet butter. *Oi,* such pleasure!

## Pumpernickel

This delicious heavy black bread used to be readily available at most Jewish bakeries. It still is, but modern baking methods have produced a bread whose taste and texture leave much to be desired. You'd have to go a long way to find a better pumpernickel than you can make with this recipe.

*2 packages active dry yeast*
*½ cup lukewarm water*
*¼ teaspoon sugar*
*1 cup black coffee*
*1 tablespoon corn oil*
*2 squares (2 ounces)*
*   unsweetened chocolate*

*⅓ cup molasses*
*1 tablespoon kosher salt*
*2½ cups rye flour*
*3 cups unbleached flour*
*Cornmeal*

Dissolve yeast in ½ cup warm water with ¼ teaspoon sugar. In a small, heavy saucepan combine the coffee, oil, chocolate, and molasses. Simmer, stirring, over low heat until the chocolate is completely melted. Remove from heat and let cool to lukewarm.

In a large mixing bowl combine the melted chocolate and coffee mixture with the dissolved yeast. Stir in the salt and rye flour and mix with an electric mixer. Gradually beat in the unbleached flour, adding no more than 1 cup at a time to make a workable dough. Remove the dough to a lightly floured surface and knead for about 10 minutes, adding additional unbleached flour as necessary, until dough is smooth and elastic. The dough will feel very heavy.

Place the dough in an oiled bowl, rub the top with oil, and cover with a clean towel. Set aside in a warm place to rise until it has doubled in bulk, 1½ to 2 hours.

Punch down the dough, knead briefly, and divide into two equal portions. Shape into round or oval loaves. Oil a baking sheet, sprinkle with cornmeal, and place loaves on baking sheet. Cover with a towel and let rise in a warm place until they have doubled in bulk, 45 to 60 minutes.

Preheat oven to 375°F.

Bake in a preheated oven for 35 to 45 minutes. Loaves should sound hollow when tapped on the bottom with your knuckles. Let cool on wire racks.

Y IELD :  *2 loaves.*

*Advice from Mama:*   To make raisin pumpernickel, soak ¼ cup raisins overnight or cook for a few minutes in boiling water. Drain. When raisins are cooled add them at the same time as the coffee and melted chocolate.

# Challah

Momma's home-baked challah was so arranged that you didn't have to slice it. There were bulges all around which you just pulled out of their sockets with ease and *toonked* into nice, oily soup with big eyes that looked up at you from the plate.
—*Sam Levenson*

To me, the word "challah" (please don't pronounce it "holly") evokes memories of Friday-night Sabbath dinners. When I think of challah, I remember family, love, warmth, and newspapers spread out on the just-cleaned kitchen floor. (To protect it from muddy feet, dummy!) If I go on thinking about it, I get to French toast, the fat golden slices slathered with fresh sweet butter or grieben. Or just a big thick slice of golden challah used as a sop for gravy.

Challah is, of course, full of symbolism that is more than just personal. It is customary for two loaves of challah to be placed on the Sabbath table. They are not to be cut until after the blessing has been said. The two loaves recall the memory of the wilderness, where God sent a double portion of manna on Friday.

In the past there were many different shapes given to the challah, though today it is almost always braided for the Sabbath and the other shapes are reserved for holidays. For example, challah is made round for Rosh Hashana to symbolize the calendar coming full circle and flowing into the New Year. Sometimes it is shaped into ladders to symbolize the steps to heaven.

In the old days, back in the shtetl, a woman was judged by the taste and beauty of her challah. Naturally the judges were all the other women. Each housewife brought her unbaked challah to the village baker (who had the only oven around) in preparation for the Sabbath. Each would look at the challahs of the other women and derive great pleasure in being able to criticize, thinking full well that her own was the best.

*2 packages active dry yeast*
*2½ cups lukewarm water*
*½ cup sugar*
*1 tablespoon kosher salt*

*½ cup corn oil or safflower oil*
*5 eggs*
*6 to 8 cups all-purpose flour*

In a large mixing bowl sprinkle the yeast over 2½ cups of lukewarm water and add 1 tablespoon sugar. Let stand for 10 minutes until mixture becomes frothy. Add remaining sugar, salt, corn or safflower oil, and 4 eggs. Beat well to mix. Gradually add 6 cups flour, stirring to mix well. You should have a very soft, pliable dough. If dough looks too wet, add a little more flour, enough to make it hold together. Turn the dough out on a lightly floured work surface and knead, adding additional flour until you have a very elastic dough that is not sticky. This should take 15 to 20 minutes. Wash and dry the bowl and rub the inside with corn oil. Place the dough in the bowl, cover with a towel, and let stand in a warm place for 1½ to 2 hours, until dough has doubled in bulk.

Remove the dough to a lightly floured surface and knead for a few minutes until dough feels smooth and elastic. For 1 large challah, divide the dough into 7 equal pieces. Roll each piece into a rope approximately 12 to 14 inches long. Place 4 ropes on the prepared baking sheet and pinch all the ends of one side together. Neatly braid the 4 ropes, pinching ends together at the other end. Make a braid of the remaining 3 ropes and place this braid carefully on top of the first braid. For 2 smaller challahs, divide the dough into 6 equal pieces and roll into ropes about 14 inches long. Braid 3 ropes together to make 2 challahs. Cover and let rise in a warm place until doubled in bulk, about 1 hour.

Preheat oven to 375°F. Lightly grease a baking sheet with vegetable oil.

Beat the remaining egg together with 1 tablespoon water and brush it all over the challah. Bake for 45 to 50 minutes, until challah is golden brown and sounds hollow when tapped on the bottom. Let cool before slicing.

YIELD: *1 large or 2 medium challahs.*

## Pletzel (Flat Onion Bread)

Onion pletzel is about one of my favorite breads. Spread with cream cheese or sweet butter, it's heavenly. It also makes a deliciously different hors d'oeuvres bread when cut into small squares. It has lots of *tam* (taste) without overwhelming whatever you serve with it.

*1 package active dry yeast*   *¼ cup lukewarm water*
*1 teaspoon sugar*             *1 cup water*

| | |
|---|---|
| *1 cup milk* | *5 to 6 cups flour* |
| *2 tablespoons corn or safflower* | *1 egg, beaten* |
| *  oil* | *1 cup finely chopped onion* |
| *2 teaspoons kosher salt* | *Kosher salt* |

Dissolve yeast and sugar in ¼ cup warm water. In a small saucepan combine 1 cup water, 1 cup milk, and corn or safflower oil. Heat until warm, but do not boil. Pour the milk into a large mixing bowl and mix with dissolved yeast. Stir in salt and gradually stir in flour to make a soft, workable dough. Remove to a lightly floured surface and knead for 10 minutes, until dough is smooth and elastic. Place the dough in an oiled bowl, cover with a clean towel, and let rise in a warm place until it has doubled in bulk, 1 to 1½ hours.

Lightly grease two baking sheets with vegetable oil.

Punch down dough and knead briefly on a lightly floured surface. Divide the dough into 4 equal pieces and roll each piece into a ball. Flatten and roll out each ball into a large, flat board about ½ inch thick. Place pletzel on prepared baking sheets. Cover with a clean towel and let rise until doubled in bulk, 45 to 60 minutes.

Preheat oven to 375°F.

Brush the pletzel boards with beaten egg and sprinkle with chopped onion and kosher salt. Bake in preheated oven for 20 to 30 minutes, until onions are golden brown and the edges of the pletzel are crispy and light brown.

YIELD:   *4 pletzel onion breads.*


# Zemmel (Rolls)

I think of zemmel as the Jewish version of white bread rolls, but what a delicious difference. Zemmel are nice and crusty on the outside and soft and chewy on the inside. Take my word, you can't buy rolls like this anywhere, not when you want to eat them still warm out of the oven the way my mother and I used to when I was a little girl. I would dunk my warm zemmel in my milk and she would dunk hers in a glass of light coffee. Whether you eat them hot with butter, or dunk them, or use them to make a sandwich—homemade zemmel are pure heaven.

| | |
|---|---|
| 1 package active dry yeast | 2 teaspoons kosher salt |
| 1 teaspoon sugar | 5 to 6 cups flour |
| 1/4 cup lukewarm water | 1 egg, beaten |
| 1 cup water | Poppy or sesame seeds |
| 1 cup milk | |
| 2 tablespoons corn or safflower oil | |

Dissolve yeast and sugar in 1/4 cup warm water. In a small saucepan combine 1 cup water, 1 cup milk, and corn or safflower oil. Heat until warm, but do not boil. Pour the milk mixture into a large mixing bowl and mix with dissolved yeast. Stir in salt and gradually stir in flour to make a soft, workable dough. Remove to a lightly floured surface and knead for 10 minutes, until dough is smooth and elastic. Place the dough in an oiled bowl, cover with a clean towel, and let rise in a warm place until it has doubled in bulk, 1 to 1½ hours.

Lightly grease a baking sheet with vegetable shortening.

Punch down dough and knead briefly on a lightly floured surface. Divide the dough into 16 to 18 equal pieces and roll each piece into a ball. Flatten each ball into a round about 3 inches in diameter and 1 inch thick. Place flattened rounds on prepared baking sheet, 2 inches apart. Make a deep crease with the dull side of a knife down the center of each roll. Cover with a clean towel and let rise until rolls have doubled in bulk, 45 to 60 minutes.

Preheat oven to 375°F.

Brush rolls with beaten egg and sprinkle with poppy or sesame seeds. Bake in preheated oven for 20 minutes, until rolls are crisp and lightly browned.

YIELD: *16 to 18 rolls.*

# Onion Zemmel

1 package active dry yeast
1 teaspoon sugar
¼ cup lukewarm water
1 cup water
1 cup milk
2 tablespoons corn or safflower
  oil

2 teaspoons kosher salt
5 to 6 cups flour
1 egg, beaten
1 cup finely chopped onion
Kosher salt

Dissolve yeast and sugar in ¼ cup warm water. In a small saucepan combine 1 cup water, 1 cup milk, and corn or safflower oil. Heat until warm, but do not boil. Pour the milk mixture into a large mixing bowl and mix with dissolved yeast. Stir in salt and gradually stir in flour to make a soft, workable dough. Remove to a lightly floured surface and knead for 10 minutes, until dough is smooth and elastic. Place the dough in an oiled bowl, cover with a clean towel, and let rise in a warm place until it has doubled in bulk, 1 to 1½ hours.

Lightly grease a baking sheet with vegetable shortening.

Punch down dough and knead briefly on a lightly floured surface. Divide the dough into 14 to 16 equal pieces and roll each piece into a ball. Flatten each ball into a round about 4 inches in diameter and ½ inch thick. Place flattened rounds on prepared baking sheet 2 inches apart. Make a deep crease with the dull side of a knife down the center of each roll. Cover with a clean towel and let rise until rolls have doubled in bulk, 45 to 60 minutes.

Preheat oven to 375°F.

Brush rolls with beaten egg and sprinkle with 1 to 2 teaspoons chopped onion and a little kosher salt. Bake in preheated oven for 20 to 25 minutes, until rolls are lightly browned and onions are golden brown.

YIELD: *14 to 16 rolls.*

# Bagels

❖

In the mythical village of Chelm, the town of fools, the town council once decided that they needed to learn how to make bagels. So they sent a delegation to Vilna, because Vilna was famous for its fine bagels. They found the foremost baker and told him that they were willing to pay him a good price to teach them how to make bagels. The baker told them that there was nothing simpler. "Take some round holes," he said, "not too big, not too small. Put some dough around them, simmer them in a pot of hot water, then bake them in the oven until they're nice and done." Well, you can try his recipe, or you can try mine. It's up to you.

*5 to 6 cups all-purpose flour*          *3 tablespoons sugar or honey*
*2½ teaspoons kosher salt*               *5 tablespoons corn oil*
*1 package active dry yeast*             *2 eggs*
*1¼ cups lukewarm water*                 *5 to 6 quarts water*

In a large mixing bowl combine 2 cups of flour with the salt and yeast. Stir in the lukewarm water and sugar or honey. Add the oil and eggs and beat with an electric mixer until the mixture is very smooth. Add the flour, 1 cup at a time, to make a soft but workable dough. Remove the dough to a lightly floured surface and knead for about 10 minutes, until dough is smooth and elastic. Wash, dry, and oil the inside of the mixing bowl and replace the dough in the bowl. Cover and let rise at room temperature until the dough has doubled in bulk (1 to 1½ hours).

Punch down the dough, remove to a lightly floured surface, and knead briefly. Divide the dough into 20 to 24 equal pieces. Roll each piece of dough into a log 6 inches long and approximately ¾ inch thick. Pinch the ends together to make a round bagel. Place the shaped bagels on a lightly floured board, cover with a towel, and let rise for another 45 minutes.

Set the water to boil in a large pot. Preheat oven to 375°F. Lightly grease a cookie sheet with corn oil.

Use a spatula to slide the bagels into gently boiling water. As bagels float to the top, turn them over and simmer for 3 minutes longer. Remove from water with a large slotted spoon and place on prepared cookie sheet. Bake at 375°F for 10 minutes, then increase temperature to 400°F and bake for an additional 10 to 15 minutes, until bagels are golden brown and crisp.

YIELD:   *20 to 24 bagels.*

*Advice from Mama:*

1. Just before baking, brush the bagels with an egg white that has been beaten with 1 tablespoon water. Sprinkle the bagels with your choice of either kosher salt, poppy seeds, sesame seeds, finely chopped onion, or finely chopped garlic.
2. Serve freshly baked bagels with cream cheese, Nova Scotia salmon, whitefish chubs, or kippered (baked) salmon. My friend Ruth loves bagels with sable. If you've never tried this combination, do so, because it is delicious. A nice breakfast!

# 14

# SWEETS

□ □ □ □ □ □ □ □ □ □ □ □ □ □ □ □ □ □ □ □ □

For *everyday eating,* according to my mother, the best dessert was a piece of fresh fruit. And who can argue with her about that? If she wanted to get fancy, instead of having a plain apple, she would bake it. For even more special, she would make a fruit compote.

For really special occasions, she would roll up her sleeves and make mandelbrot, rugalach, or hamantaschen. In my mother's world view these pastries were baked to impress and entertain other ladies. Oh, sure, the family always got to eat them as well, but the family had to make do with what she considered to be the rejects: broken cookies, pastries slightly burned around the edges, hamantaschen that weren't shaped quite right. The perfect cookies were kept strictly for company.

Anyway, if you're looking for chocolate mousse or orange soufflé, go look them up in Julia Child. If you want what your *bubbe* (grandmother) made for your mother or you, then look no further.

# Baked Apples

If you were to ask anyone of my generation to name a typical Jewish dessert that they were served at home, you'd probably hear "baked apples."

There are a lot of reasons for this: they were easy to prepare, inexpensive, and, more important, healthy! But just because all this is true is no reason to look down your nose at a good baked apple. If you've never served them to your family and friends, do me a favor. Try this recipe. You'll find they disappear very quickly. Also, a leftover baked apple for breakfast is a very good thing.

Let's not forget that going back all the way to the Old Testament, in the Song of Songs, it says, "Comfort me with apples for I am sick of love," showing that even then Jews knew about the natural goodness of an apple.

*6 large red baking apples*
*Juice of 1 lemon*
*¹/₂ cup brown sugar*
*1 tablespoon cornstarch*
*1 cup orange or pineapple juice*

*2 tablespoons unsalted butter or*
   *margarine*
*¹/₂ teaspoon powdered*
   *cinnamon (optional)*

Preheat oven to 350°F.

Core the apples and peel away the skin one-third of the way down. Sprinkle with fresh lemon juice to prevent browning. Place peeled side up in an ovenproof dish or pan.

In a small saucepan combine brown sugar, cornstarch, and orange or pineapple juice. Bring to a boil, reduce heat, and simmer, stirring frequently, until the mixture thickens and becomes clear (about 10 minutes). Spoon this mixture into the hollowed-out part

of the apple and spoon some over the entire apple to coat generously. Dot each apple with butter or margarine and sprinkle with
cinnamon.

Bake, basting the apples once or twice, for 30 to 45 minutes, until
apples are tender. Serve apples warm from the oven or cooled to
room temperature.

YIELD:   *6 baked apples.*

*Advice from Mama:*   I have baked all sorts of apples over the
years and found that all of them in their own way are delicious.
But if you can get them, Rome Beauties are especially good for
baking.

# Dried Fruit Compote

Every good Jewish household had two desserts that appeared with
clockwork regularity—baked apples and fruit compote. Both were
considered healthy and "good for your stomach," whatever that
meant. For years after I was married and away from home, I
wouldn't even attempt to make a compote because I had grown so
sick of it and was now finally free to choose my own desserts. But
as I got older I started to yearn for a good compote and this recipe
evolved. So give it a try and let me know how you like it.

*2 pounds mixed dried fruits*
  *(prunes, apricots, pineapple,*
  *pears, and figs)*
*1/2 cup orange juice*
*1/2 cup water*

*1 tablespoon lemon juice*
*6 cloves*
*1 stick cinnamon (or 1/2*
  *teaspoon powdered cinnamon)*
*1/2 cup brown sugar*

Soak dried fruits in cold water to cover overnight. Drain the
fruit and place in a saucepan together with the orange juice, water,
lemon juice, cloves, and cinnamon. Simmer gently for 45 minutes,

then add sugar and cook, stirring frequently, for 10 minutes longer. Serve cooled to room temperature or chilled.

YIELD: *8 to 10 servings.*

*Advice from Mama:* A nice variation is to substitute ½ cup honey for the sugar. This makes for a different kind of sweetness.

# Bread Pudding

From the old country came the idea of not ever wasting anything that was edible, and the one thing that was never, ever wasted was bread of any kind. And as every good cook knows, from this idea of not wasting have come some of the best, most delicious dishes imaginable. Bread pudding is in this category. In my whole life I've never met anyone who didn't like bread pudding. Try serving it for dessert at your fanciest party. However much you make, it won't be enough.

You can make this bread pudding using any leftover bread you have, but somehow I think stale challah gives it the best flavor. For a parve dessert use margarine and substitute orange juice for the milk. Also very delicious.

*3 eggs*
*⅓ cup brown sugar*
*¼ teaspoon salt*
*½ teaspoon cinnamon*
*1 teaspoon vanilla extract or 1 tablespoon orange liqueur*

*4 tablespoons unsalted butter or margarine*
*2 cups milk or orange juice*
*2½ cups stale bread (preferably challah), cut into 1-inch cubes*
*½ cup raisins (optional)*

Preheat oven to 350°F.
In a bowl whisk together the eggs, sugar, salt, cinnamon, and vanilla extract or orange liqueur. In a saucepan melt the butter or

margarine, add the milk or juice, and let heat just to lukewarm. Remove from flame and mix together with the stale bread. Add egg mixture and stir well. If you are using raisins or any dried fruit, toss the fruit together with 1 tablespoon flour and fold into the pudding mixture. (Coating with flour prevents the fruit from settling on the bottom.) Transfer the mixture to a well-greased oven-proof casserole or baking dish and place this casserole or dish into a larger pan. Pour boiling water into the larger pan to 1 inch below top rim. Bake in preheated oven for approximately 1 hour, or until a sharp knife inserted in the middle comes out clean.

YIELD: *4 to 6 servings.*

*Advice from Mama:* A combination of chopped pitted prunes, apricots, and raisins makes this an even more festive dessert.

# Mandelbrot
# (Almond Bread Cookies)

These are delicious when they are slightly soft, but some people love them better when they become crunchy hard. Mandelbrot will stay soft if you store them in an airtight container. If you would like to have them crisp and crunchy, they will harden if exposed to the air and allowed to dry out.

*⅓ cup corn oil, butter, or*
 *margarine*
*½ cup sugar*
*3 eggs*
*4 tablespoons orange juice*
*1 teaspoon lemon juice*

*½ teaspoon vanilla extract*
*½ cup blanched almonds,*
 *coarsely chopped*
*2 cups all-purpose flour*
*2 teaspoons baking powder*
*Pinch of salt*

Preheat oven to 350°F. Grease a baking sheet with vegetable oil, dust with flour, turn upside down and shake off any excess.

In a bowl cream together oil, butter, or margarine with the sugar until light and fluffy. Beat in eggs, one at a time, until mixture is light and frothy. Beat in orange juice, lemon juice, and vanilla extract. Stir in almonds. Sift together the flour, baking powder, and salt. Gradually stir in flour mixture to make a soft, workable dough. Remove to a lightly floured surface and knead until dough is smooth and elastic, about 10 minutes. Divide in two and shape each piece into a loaf approximately 3 inches wide by 2 inches thick. Place on prepared baking sheet and bake for about 30 minutes, until the loaves are lightly browned. Remove from oven and let cool until just warm. Cut each loaf into ½-inch slices.

YIELD:   *24 to 28 pieces mandelbrot.*

# Rugalach

If you were to offer your parents or grandparents a choice for dessert, say chocolate fudge cake or rugalach, rugalach would win hands down. These wonderful little pastries are delicious and satisfying, either as an afternoon treat or at the end of a meal, without being cloyingly sweet. And if you can keep from eating more than a couple, they're not all that fattening, either. Rugalach last for weeks if wrapped well and refrigerated, and for months if frozen.

I have come across rugalach made with other ingredients, including raisins, prunes, whatever. I'm not saying they're not good, but this version is the only one I ever make, and by me it's the best.

*½ cup unsalted butter*              *1 egg*
*4 ounces cream cheese*              *1 tablespoon water*
*½ cup sour cream*                   *2 tablespoons sugar*
*1½ cups all-purpose flour*          *1 tablespoon powdered*
*½ cup raspberry or apricot jam*        *cinnamon*
*¼ cup chopped walnuts*

In the bowl of an electric mixer combine the butter and cream cheese. Cream together until well blended, then blend in sour cream. Gradually beat in the flour to make a soft dough. Divide the dough in two, roll into balls, wrap in plastic wrap, and refrigerate for several hours or overnight.

Preheat oven to 350°F. Grease a baking sheet with vegetable oil.

Roll out each ball of dough on a lightly floured surface into a rectangle 12 inches long by 4 inches wide. Spread the jam on rolled-out dough and sprinkle lightly with walnuts. Roll the dough up along the wide edge into a log and place end side down. In a small bowl beat the egg together with 1 tablespoon water. Brush the top of the dough with the beaten egg and sprinkle with a mixture of sugar and cinnamon. Cut each log into 12 1-inch pieces and place them on prepared baking sheet. Bake for 20 to 30 minutes, or until lightly browned.

YIELD: *24 rugalach.*

# Hamantaschen

My entire family always thought that my mother made the best hamantaschen and I was always sure that this was a recipe that had been handed down to her from generations of great hamantaschen bakers. When I asked her to tell me about the origins of this family recipe, she laughed and replied, "No, *mamala,* I got this recipe while talking to a neighbor. It sounded so much better than your *bubbe*'s yeast dough hamantaschen." So much for the romance of family recipes. Still, the way the recipe was given to me, it was very much a *schit arein* and *yohrzeit-*glass recipe. The glass was used for both measuring and cutting out the rounds of dough. It wasn't until I had to pass it on to my own daughter that I had to figure out the more definite amounts.

My son, Bennett, and I prefer the prune filling, but my daughter, Robin, prefers the poppy seed or apricot filling. Make your own choice, you can't go wrong.

½ cup sugar
½ cup corn oil
2 eggs
3 tablespoons orange or
    pineapple juice
3 cups flour

1½ teaspoons baking powder
¼ teaspoon salt
Hamantaschen filling of your
    choice (pages 242 to 246)
1 egg, beaten together with 1
    tablespoon water (optional)

In the large bowl of an electric mixer, beat the sugar and oil until well blended. Beat in eggs, one at a time, until mixture is very light and frothy, then beat in orange or pineapple juice. Sift together flour, baking powder, and salt and gradually beat into the liquid mixture until you have a soft but workable dough. Remove to a lightly floured surface and knead into a ball.

Preheat oven to 375°F. Brush several cookie sheets with oil.

Divide the dough into 6 to 8 pieces for easier handling. While you are rolling and cutting one piece, keep the others covered with a towel so they don't dry out. Flatten each piece of dough with the palm of your hand and then roll out with a rolling pin to a ¼-inch thickness. Use a 3½-inch cookie cutter or the rim of a wide-mouthed glass to cut out circles of dough. Place a heaping teaspoon of your favorite filling in the center of each round. Fold 3 edges of each round over the filling, bringing them together to make a triangle. Pinch these folds together, leaving a little of the filling showing.

Place each hamantaschen on prepared cookie sheet, about ¼ inch apart. Brush with beaten egg if desired (this gives the finished hamantaschen more color). Bake in a preheated oven for 10 to 15 minutes or until golden brown. Cool on wire racks. Continue baking until all are done.

YIELD: *55 to 60 hamantaschen.*

# Prune Filling for Hamantaschen

The best lekvar (prune filling) I have ever tasted comes from Paprikas Weiss. And luckily for everybody who doesn't live in New York City, you can buy from them mail-order.

Paprikas Weiss
1546 Second Avenue
New York, New York 10028
(212) 288-6117

*3 cups or 3 8-ounce jars of*
  *lekvar (prune filling)*

*1 cup walnuts or pecans,*
  *crushed (optional)*

This prepared filling is delicious and I think that making your own from scratch is a waste of time and effort. If you feel guilty doing something so easy as to take a filling straight from a jar, stir in 1 cup of crushed walnuts or pecans.

If you really want to make your own from scratch, here's how:

*1 cup raisins*
*1 15-ounce jar cooked pitted*
  *prunes, drained*
*¼ cup sugar or honey*

*1 teaspoon lemon juice*
*1 cup crushed walnuts or pecans*
  *(optional)*

In a small bowl add water to the raisins to cover and let soak overnight. Combine prunes, drained raisins, sugar or honey, and lemon juice in the bowl of a food processor and blend to a fine paste. Remove to a mixing bowl and stir in the crushed nuts if you are using them. Cover and refrigerate for several hours or overnight. This mixture is easier to handle when it is cold.

YIELD:  *3 to 4 cups.*

# Mohn or Poppy Seed Filling for Hamantaschen

꧁

*1 cup ground poppy seeds*
*1 cup milk*
*1 cup seedless raisins*
*2 tablespoons honey*
*1/2 teaspoon vanilla extract*

*2 tablespoons corn oil*
*1 teaspoon lemon rind*
*1/2 cup chopped walnuts or*
*   pecans*

If you cannot get ground poppy seeds, you can grind your own in a clean coffee grinder or food processor. Grind them to a fine, smooth texture but not a paste.

In a saucepan combine ground poppy seeds, milk, raisins, and honey. Bring to a boil and cook over medium heat, stirring frequently, until the mixture thickens. Cool and stir in vanilla extract, corn oil, lemon rind, and chopped walnuts or pecans. Chill thoroughly in the refrigerator before filling hamantaschen.

Y I E L D :  *Approximately 3 cups.*

<u>*Advice from Mama:*</u>  Poppy seeds, ground poppy seeds, and a very good prepared poppy seed filling are also all available from:

Paprikas Weiss
1546 Second Avenue
New York, New York 10028
(212) 288-6117

# Apricot Filling for Hamantaschen

––––––––––––  ♥  ––––––––––––

3 cups apricot preserves
Juice of 1 lemon

¼ cup toasted chopped walnuts
  (optional)

Mix apricot preserves, lemon juice, and nuts together.

YIELD:  3 cups.


# Viennese Kugelhopf or Coffee Cake

––––––––––––  ♥  ––––––––––––

1 package active dry yeast
¼ cup warm milk
1 tablespoon sugar
½ pound unsalted butter or
  margarine
¾ cup confectioners' sugar
3 egg yolks
2½ cups flour

¼ teaspoon salt
¾ cup milk
1 cup raisins
1 cup chopped pecans or
  walnuts
1 tablespoon grated lemon rind
Additional confectioners' sugar
  for topping

Dissolve the yeast in ¼ cup warm milk together with 1 tablespoon sugar.

In the bowl of an electric mixer, combine the butter or margarine and the confectioners' sugar. Beat together until mixture is very light and fluffy. Beat in egg yolks and continue beating until mixture is a very light lemon color. Mix in the flour and salt, adding it alternately with the ¾ cup milk. Finally beat in the yeast mixture and continue beating until completely blended. Fold in the raisins, nuts, and lemon rind.

Grease a 6-cup kugelhopf mold or a 10-inch tube pan with butter or margarine. Place the dough in it, cover with a towel, and let rise in a warm place for about 1 hour, or until doubled in bulk.

Preheat oven to 375°F.

When dough has risen, bake in preheated oven for 45 to 50 minutes, or until cake tester comes out clean. Let cool in pan for about 15 minutes, then invert the cake onto a plate. Cover with a towel and let cool completely. Sprinkle with confectioners' sugar and serve.

This cake tastes even better the next day or the day after.

YIELD: *8 to 10 servings.*

# Honey Cake (Lekach)

Everyone knows that in the Bible ancient Israel is always referred to as the Land of Milk and Honey. Until the Middle Ages honey was the main sweetener used throughout Europe and the Middle East. Recipes for cakes and other sweets made with honey are as ancient as the Bible and still as popular as they ever were.

| | |
|---|---|
| *1 orange* | *¹/₂ teaspoon ground cloves* |
| *1 cup brown sugar* | *¹/₂ teaspoon ground cinnamon* |
| *4 eggs* | *¹/₂ teaspoon salt* |
| *1 16-ounce jar honey* | *³/₄ cup black coffee* |
| *¹/₄ cup corn oil or safflower oil* | *1 cup pitted prunes, cut in half* |
| *3¹/₂ cups flour* | *¹/₂ cup raisins* |
| *1¹/₂ tablespoons baking powder* | *¹/₂ cup chopped walnuts or* |
| *1 teaspoon baking soda* | *pecans* |

Quarter the orange, remove any visible seeds, and grind it together with the peel in a food processor or electric grinder.

In a bowl beat together the sugar and eggs until very light and frothy. Add honey, oil, and ground orange and beat well. In a separate bowl sift together 3 cups of flour, baking powder, baking soda, cloves, cinnamon, and salt. Gradually beat the dry ingredients into the honey mixture alternately with the black coffee until well blended.

Preheat oven to 350°F. Grease the insides of two 9-by-5-inch bread pans with oil and line the bottom with parchment paper.

Mix the remaining ½ cup flour together with the prunes, raisins, and nuts. Fold gently into the cake batter. Spoon the batter into the prepared pans. Bake for approximately 1 hour. To test if the cake is done, insert a toothpick into the center. If it comes out clean, the cake is done. If not, bake for an additional 15 minutes. Let cool in pans. Remove when cool, peel away parchment paper, and wrap tightly in plastic wrap. If you are planning to keep the honey cake more than a few weeks, refrigerate. The honey cake will keep several weeks without refrigeration and tastes better after it has ripened a few days.

YIELD:   *2 honey cakes.*

# 15

# AROUND *the* KITCHEN TABLE: FINAL THOUGHTS *from* MAMA LEAH

S ometimes it seems to me that all of the really important events of my life have taken place around the kitchen. And if that's not quite exactly true then at least the kitchen table always provided a place to talk, cry, or laugh about them. In many ways the kitchen has been my life.

When I was a child my mother cooked there and my father read the paper and complained about the political news. Friends and relatives visited, bringing gossip and coffee cake, and we kids did our homework, played games, or listened to the radio. Losses small and great were grieved at the kitchen table. Good news, petty or grand, was celebrated there.

When I was older and going out on dates, if I liked the boy, I invited him in when he brought me home, and together we'd raid the icebox and end our evening around that kitchen table. And after the boy went home my Papa would sometimes emerge shyly from the shadows of the darkened apartment, and we would sit awhile longer at the kitchen table, sharing as much as it was possible for father and daughter to share.

Stan Fischer, my husband of thirty-two years, proposed to me at the kitchen table, while we were having coffee. That night we sat so long that finally my mother and father joined us and wished us a Mazel Tov!

When Stan and I had a kitchen of our own, that was just naturally where the family and friends convened several times a day for meals, of course, but also to knosh and schmooz, to kvetch and kvell. There I paid the bills, or else worried about not having enough to pay the bills. That was where my children did their homework, and where a new set of joys and sorrows were savored.

When the restaurant was finally opened the kitchen was my office, and now that Stanley is gone and the kids grown up, the kitchen is my haven, my place of meditation and solace.

Finally, now, I've written this book and it's not a fancy book (Jewish cooking is not a fancy cuisine)—it's not a coffee table book, it's (you guessed it) a kitchen table book. That venerable and homely item of furniture was really the only possible and proper desk for the job, and I like to picture you, the reader, sitting at your kitchen table as you read it, as you use it. Good appetite and happy cooking.

# INDEX